FINDING MY REAL FATHER

MY JOURNEY WITH GOD
TO THE ENDS OF THE EARTH

JAMES BOWMAN

outskirts
press

Endorsements

In *Finding My Real Father,* Jim Bowman tells a story you don't want to miss. His compelling memoir moves from the dead-end of high-level crime—the world his father knew—to the incredible kingdom of God, where his true Father is about the business of redemption. In Bowman's life, including the development of the enormously fruitful ministry of Scriptures in Use, we see a vibrant example of the leading of God in the lives of those who seek him. A powerful and deeply encouraging book.

Warren Walsh, Editorial Director, YWAM Publishing

———◆———

Jim Bowman pulls back the curtain on his life and lets us journey with him as he searches for a father. While his biological father let him down, not so his heavenly Father. This page-turner reveals how God prepared a servant to reach the unreached of the oral world at home and abroad. This is a story that makes Jesus famous over and over again.

Tom Steffen, professor emeritus,
Cook School of Intercultural Studies, Biola University

———◆———

Jim Bowman's compelling journey is a story that deserves attention. Growing up with an absent father led Jim on a long and winding search for the ultimate relationship of his life. His writing reflects the authentic person of faith I have come to know. This book gives insight into such amazing grace that positioned Jim to become one of the key catalysts for world evangelization in our generation.

Rick Sessoms, President, Freedom to Lead

———— ♦ ————

Abandoned by his natural father, Jim had to learn how to forgive and love until he was abandoned to his heavenly father. Only then did God use his life to testify of His love and forgiveness to unreached, non-reading people groups across the globe though translation, film and oral strategy. His amazing work and testimony continues through SIU and the foundations, relationships, and vision he and Carla established forty years ago.

Doug Seaver, Firm Foundation

———— ♦ ————

Jim Bowman has an amazing and engaging story to tell about his life. His father, a famous diamond thief, abandons his family and his son in the pursuit of worldly treasures. God as Jim's heavenly father embraces Jim with love and tenderness and yet calls him to be a soldier in the Lord's army to fight evil, spiritual darkness, poverty, ignorance and suffering. Out of the ashes comes a man of honor, out of the counter culture comes a downwardly mobile Kingdom man who cares about lifting up the lost, least and last of this world. Jim's life touches the whole world as he partners with an awesome wife and other missional people called to make a difference in this world. I have known Jim for many years and been amazed at what God has done. This is an inspirational story!

Randy Reynolds,
pastor, counselor, author, community developer and servant of God.

I thought it a love story in so many ways. Jim's love and desire for a relationship with God. His true love and respect for his wife Carla. A love for Maureen and his daughters, his love for the poor, and love for the Gospel are apparent. Jim's story is compelling and inspirational, thought provoking and a wonderful invitation to choose God as your savior and friend.

Pam Vannelli missions advocate

This book has provided leading and direction for my own life, giving me a clearer path to follow. It has inspired in me faith and confidence that at this stage of life, God can still fulfill the promises and hopes He instilled in my heart. I am encouraged that my dreams will one day be fulfilled.

Gary Lovelace. Envoy Foundation

———— ◆ ————

This is a great adventure story of a man looking for the love of a father. That alone is reason to read it, but it is so much more than a deep father-wound tale. It is a look inside a critical part of the movement of God to reach unreached, oral peoples. We learn how the story of Jesus is being told to oral communicators all over the world. This book also provides great insight to what finding faith in Jesus looked like in the 1960's and 1970's. Jim's narritive both inspires and gives practical spiritual lessons anyone can apply. It has been an honor to travel with and support Jim and Carla as they followed God's leading to make a huge difference in our world.

Glen Elliott, Lead Pastor, Pantano Christian Church

———— ◆ ————

Reading Jim's story of his search for a loving Father reminds me of *I Dare to Call Him Father*. I first became aware of Jim through his work in North India with S.D. Ponraj. There is a saying "like father like son", but in Jim's case God's Spirit did a totally new work in him. He and Carla have been pioneers in communicating the Gospel to oral people groups. His personal story shows the depths God goes to in order to comfort and redeem so that the earth might be filled with the knowledge of the Glory of God.

Cody Watson, Associate Director Frontier Fellowship

---◆---

I was deeply moved as I read the account of Jim's journey with his true Father, the lessons he learned about life, love, and trust and of the way his life opened new doors of evangelism and discipleship by honoring oral cultures and by simply telling them the stories of Jesus. This book is a treasure on many levels. Enjoy!

Dan Gill, Senior Pastor emeritus, Abundant Life Christian Center

Table of Contents

Foreword

I first met Jim Bowman on a Skype call in 2014 when the SIU Board Search Committee was looking for a successor and replacement for the SIU Executive Director and CEO position. Jim was extremely gracious and humble in every way. The Board wanted him to give his recommendation on the candidates they were interviewing (and rightfully so). It is not easy to replace a God fearing man and pioneering disciple-maker like Jim Bowman. I was actually the third choice of the candidates but Jim immediately knew I was different. He was confident that the Lord would equip me and lead me in His direction. This would be His organization IF I were willing to submit my dreams and desires to the Lord.

I've come to cherish this man deeply as he (and his wife, Carla) have taken me under their wings and mentored me all along the way. The transition from a founder-led organization to one that we have now – one that continues to flourish in the harvest fields around the world with courageous indigenous men and women of peace- is truly an act of God and miracle. I believe that the grace and humility of both Jim and Carla releasing the next season of SIU's future to the Lord, to a new leader, and a new team was part of an amazing miracle...a successful founder transition. This new team seeks the Lord, collaborates and learns together and has forged ahead for a strong future.

As for the story that you are about to read, even Hollywood can't craft as uplifting, inspiring and supernatural a narrative as Jim Bowman's account of **"Finding My Real Father"**. God is the master storyteller and that's why they call it "HIStory", as it's "HIS Story". Jim's story is truly not of this earth. From tragic abandonment by his lying, jewel thief of a father, the son's constant heartbreak, repeated pain, this is a story of redemptive beauty. The Heavenly Father Jim meets never stops pursuing and loving his children as His adopted sons and daughters. This is the unfailing love of an indescribable, merciful, and gracious Abba, Father who reached down and grabbed Jim and as HE did so, HE has blessed the nations. We refer to what we call the "Jesus Model of the 1st Century", an important part of the orality movement that Jim and Carla Bowman helped pioneer. The God of the impossible is alive and seeking you too! Jim Bowman's life and story is clear evidence of that fact.

Kent Kiefer, Executive Director & CEO,
Scriptures In Use (SIU)

Introduction

Between the bookends of my life, childhood and old age, I traveled a long way to meet my real father, my heavenly father. Then despite the heartbreak of a fatherless, purposeless life, God met me, embraced me and instilled in me eternal purpose. My story is not a textbook case of growing up without a father or living with an absentee dad. My natural father was a handsome, charming, and endearing con artist and thief of a legendary diamond known as the Krupp Diamond and later as the Elizabeth Taylor Diamond. His continual, relentless search for wealth related directly back to the poverty of his youth in depression era West Texas. He had become obsessed with never being poor again. When reunited with my mother, my brothers and me after decades of living a double life, we hoped my dad's futile and empty quest for worldly treasure would end, but it was not to be. The attraction of evil for an essentially good man created in my dad a continual tension and inspired a doomed heist of a diamond too hot to handle. His lifestyle of crime would continue until his death.

My story was destined to be so much different. Perhaps my missing-in-action father was the catalyst for my own life choices. Perhaps the void in my life led me to passionately seek a good Father, a hero, comforting, supporting, and caring. From the backdrop of my youth, from my father's legacy of dark secrets, deception and manipulation, from heartbreak and hopelessness came restoration. God overcame all the obstacles in my life and as the loving father I never had, he embraced me and put purpose into my life. He listened, understood, and allowed me to learn by my mistakes, picking me up when ever I fell down. He wanted to spend quality time with me and he helped me overcome my past. God took me down this clear path toward redemption when I was in my twenties beginning at a Billy Graham Crusade. I joined the Jesus People Movement with all of the energy and devotion of those incredible times in our country. I was discipled and finally was called into a global ministry to unreached people. The poor, the uneducated, the ignored minorities of the world, the least understood and least reached became my best friends. My passion was for the underdog, setting the captives free, taking the Word of God to the world. How that all turned out is part of this autobiography, as is my father's ill-fated life of crime, my journey to faith, and my early years in remote villages of Latin America and Asia.

I have felt compelled to share my faith story, not only for those who are fatherless with little hope about the future, but for those who have found faith and want to live life with purpose. Too many of us doubt that ordinary people can be used by God. We assume that believers with baggage from childhood and young adulthood cannot overcome the past to serve in the Kingdom. Yet in God's economy everyone is valuable. I found out through His relentless nudging and urging that He had a purpose for my life and He did intend to use me despite the pain and abandonment I had lived through. Yes, there was so much to overcome, yes I was ordinary and untrained, but I longed to tell God's love story and to see lives transformed just as in the early days of the Apostles. I wanted to share my loving heavenly father with the world and God honored that.

I would hope my story could inspire young missions students and missionary candidates with faith that moves mountains, faith that begins movements. The Christian world may seem in decline and the church powerless with the best days behind us, but I hope this book challenges those assumptions. The best days are ahead, time to put our faith into action, to live out our faith in obedience with vision. There is still time to creatively share our faith, inspire a hunger for the Scriptures, and turn the world upside down for Jesus.

Prologue

It is the winter of 1963 in Las Vegas, Nevada. I am a senior in high school. I am at home sick when I answer the doorbell and my long lost father stands at the door, smug as you please. "Hello Jimmy, I've come home. Aren't you happy to see me?"

My father is staying at the Lee Hotel in downtown Vegas. Not exactly seedy, but not the high living he would have preferred. He's been missing for the past seven years and we have a lot of catching up to do. I am hesitant at first to even engage with the man who has left my mom, my two brothers and me in the lurch for so many years without a word. But his natural charming ways win the day as they always have and soon I am hanging out every free moment at the Lee Hotel getting re-acquainted with my father, enraptured with his stories and his great Texas drawl I hadn't heard in such a long time.

"Dad, talk to me", I say. "So much has happened in your life. I feel like I don't know anything about you." He starts his story from childhood. "I was just thirteen in 1934 and West Texas was a plain of dust. San Angelo was a hopeless town and we were hanging out by the river. One day hiding behind Aunt Sadie's clapboard house I see the government agents taking away my four sisters. I run as far away as I can and that is the beginning of my life of scams." As my dad drones on I learn of his clever and creative schemes to make a living from age ten on, his success in high school as a handsome, popular star football player who charms my mother into a long courtship and eventually marriage. I hear for the first time of the double life he led all the years of my growing up.

Finally he gets to the heist of the diamond and his time at McNeal Island. "In April of 1959 we break into the Vera Krupp ranch house outside of Vegas. After much searching we fail to find the secret safe and our hopes of millions of dollars fades. We take the diamond ring off Vera Krupp's hand and a few hundred dollars from her purse as she is held at gunpoint. Soon news of the theft is broadcast on radio and in newspapers. John Hagenson takes the diamond to Miami to court a fence from Cuba. Unfortunately Fidel Castro has recently invaded Havana from his mountain hideout and this very week has closed down the casinos and the Cuban underworld is in havoc. George Reves takes the diamond to New Jersey but the FBI has offered a reward and Reves' potential buyer calls in the feds. Reves and his wife are under arrest. As soon as they are out of jail, Mrs. Reves shoots George dead. 'You never gave me anything you promised, you swine', she declares as she raises a pistol to his head. I knew we should never have let the dames get involved. Davies and I are now wanted by the FBI but manage to evade local police in three states. We buy a big, fast car in Texas and drive to Mexico City. Picked up by the Mexican *federales* we are transported to the border where I jump into the Rio Grande as we are walking over the bridge to meet the US agents. The last ditch effort gets me nowhere. I should have stuck with gambling scams, Jimmy. I should have stuck with what I knew best."

From the moment my father sits down to tell me the story of the Krupp Diamond, everything changes for me. From Vera Krupp to Elizabeth Taylor the shocking story of my dad's involvement shakes me to the very core. A story filled with excitement and drama? Maybe. But where does that leave me, the son of a thief? I am humiliated, embarrassed and ashamed. I want to be invisible. I longed for my father's return for so many years and now I feel empty. The winds of change in our country are raging like a hurricane. Our culture is transitioning at a speed unknown before; my life seems unsettled and I am more vulnerable than I have ever been. Will I follow in his footsteps? My life is at a turning point.

1

My Dad, His Life and Times

My father, Marion Carter Bowman, was born in a small town in West Texas called San Angelo on February 19, 1921. His mother Rosa was only 14 years old when she married Lee Bowman. Soon she became pregnant with "Sonny" as she called him. Dad's father at age 21 was considerably older than Rosa and was a bootlegger with a great sense of humor. I suppose that's what attracted her to Lee.

Rosa came from a solid hard working family. Her father James Carter Aldridge was a building contractor. Her mother, Gertrude was the daughter of a lay preacher but James and Gertrude ran away together to get married against the wishes of her preacher father. Gertrude seemed to understand the crazy things we do for love.

My dad grew up in the depression era in West Texas during very hard times; the family-his father, mother and five sisters sometimes lived in a tent on the Concho River. Like for many young boys growing up during those times, selling newspapers and doing odd jobs was a way of life. Many days, he went off to school in the mornings without anything to eat except a carrot or a turnip or two he stole from a nearby garden.

From time to time, his father Lee Bowman got work as a cement worker on construction sites but the depression had no favored sons. Lee was a heavy drinker, angry and abusive. When he got work, they moved into a rented house, when work was scarce, they moved back to the river. With no food on the table my Dad did what he could to survive. In 1934 my grandfather Lee was arrested for brewing bathtub gin and bootlegging. Rosa got a day job in another town as a waitress fighting to keep her young children together; but that meant that she could only see the family on weekends. The kids bounced from family member to family member until they got tired of it all. Lee was released from jail only to learn that his sister Sadie had turned the kids over to the authorities. She wanted a more stable family environment for her own children.

"That day, Lee came home angry and he knocked me head over heels away from the table", Dad later recounted. *"My aunt had warned me earlier that day that the authorities were coming to take us away. So I said to myself, 'Well, I'll pack my little bag of clothes and "hit-em on down the road'. "I guess that I was the youngest fugitive to ever come out of Texas. When the authorities came the next day to take my sisters and me away, I was gone. I couldn't be found... and that's the way I started my life".* I would hear my dad's words, *"hit-em* on down the road", again and again through the years.

The Bowman family like so many during the depression were literally broken into little pieces. Dad's mother Rosa was in

Midland, Texas working as a waitress when all her children were taken away. Lee Bowman, as part of his parole, agreed with authorities that Dad's three younger sisters were to be sent to St. Peter and St. Joseph Catholic Covent in San Antonio. My grandmother Rosa was in Midland unaware of all that had happened. Dad's sisters stayed there at the convent until they all graduated from high school. His two baby sisters were given up for adoption. He never saw them again.

Dad, the oldest and only boy ran out the back door of Aunt Sadie's house and literally flew into the bushes. He was thirteen years old and for months he kicked around until eventually he went to live with his mother's brother Uncle Archie. Archie was just twenty years old, newly married and had plenty of his own troubles. They were hard pressed to make ends meet just like everyone else. He gave his young nephew what he could, a small room at the back of the house, but offered little guidance and direction. "Curly" was a name that stuck with him during high school. My dad stayed with his Uncle Archie until he graduated from high school in 1939.

Dad started out his life just like his own father- broken, angry and disillusioned. His newspaper job, in his way of thinking, wasn't enough. He soon learned the ways of the world to make a fast buck. One of his first scams was to buy a penny slot machine and a pair of crooked dice. Dad once said to me in that thick southern drawl I knew so well. *"I could play any game that you can name. I could put the fix on, I mean I was a cheater in dice, cards and later in life when I was golf pro I was playin' gin rummy. No way I would play unless I could cheat. The fix HAD to be on"*.

Yet, during high school Marion or "Curly", did surprisingly well.

He was an average student but an exceptional athlete. He was the star fullback for the varsity team, and he played varsity basketball and excelled on the amateur golf team. He was exceedingly handsome. People looked up to him and of course all the girls were after him. However, he was not a ladies man- he only had eyes for the beautiful Norma Ruth Clements-the one girl in his life that meant anything to him. The girl that would some day be my mother.

I am sure, that when he was a star athlete or was seen with the country club set he felt important. He needed to be recognized, admired and secretly, he needed to be loved. Everybody needs that. He certainly didn't get it at home. When I look back at my father, he had all of the advantages most kids in high school only wish they had. He was handsome and gifted with wit and cleverness. His athletic ability would later open many doors. After high school he joined the US Navy for a six-year hitch. After he enlisted, the Navy sent him to medical school. He was mustered into the 1st Marine Amphibious Corps Fleet and in 1941 served in the South Pacific during WWII as a medic at the Naval Hospital on the island of New Caledonia. He quickly rose in rank to Chief Pharmacist Mate. His medical training would later serve him well when he would falsely pose as a doctor in order to "hustle" other unsuspecting doctors into placing high stakes bets on the golf course.

It was far away in the South Pacific that Curly perfected his skills with his fellow enlisted men increasing his skills cheating at cards, dice, scams and all other manner of deception. He sent home thousands of dollars to his mother in the U.S.A. for safekeeping.

My dad was a complex man with many contradictions. In a taped interview with my dad he told me many things that would have a big impact on me: *"I guess I've done everything in the underworld or the rackets as you call it. My main objective in life was to steal, and steal for money…I was a cat burglar, a second story man, I was a good stir man, a crap dealer and a 21 dealer".* He later stated, *"All along the line I was learning my trade…and the trade I was learning was scufflin' and stealin'. That was the only way I could see that I could make it. I tried to keep this all secret, even from my wife, and I kept it a secret for many years".*

When the war was over in 1945 dad returned home to San Angelo to see his high school sweetheart Norma Ruth Clements. They were in love before he signed up to go off to war. She was the well-bred daughter of a prominent engineer and building contractor there in San Angelo. She was among the lucky ones during the depression. Her dad had money and influence in the small town of San Angelo. To the Clements family, especially Norma's mother Florence, Curly was some-one to avoid, but Norma was drawn to him like a moth to a flame.

The war years brought lots of changes. While he was in the South Pacific Curly rarely wrote Norma. Mom later told me, "I think it was against his religion to write. The truth is, he was too busy gambling during off hours." He was very non-communica-tive and secretive at his core. Norma was four years younger than Curly. She finished high school and started nurses training. Along the way, Norma had other marriage proposals, but she was holding out for the man she loved. While home on military leave Curly asked Norma to marry him after just a few dates.

However, he was the boy from the other side of the railroad tracks and Norma's mother and father were dead set against the marriage. Curly had a reputation and it wasn't a good one, but nothing was going to deter my mother from marrying the love of her life. Curly was worth any risk, worth any sacrifice. Though she came from a conservative church going family, she rejected the advice of the pastor, friends and family around her. Curly and Norma were married in a simple civil ceremony in San Angelo in December of 1945. In fact my mother rejected the church and all it represented. The church didn't offer what she was looking for.

After they were married, Curly needed to finish up his six-year stint in the Navy. After the war, he was assigned to the medical corps at the U.S. Navy Training Center in San Diego where I was born a year later in January of 1946. When he got out of the Navy, he took advantage of his GI Bill and went to college in Kilgore, Texas to finish his medical degree. After two years of pre-med he got a great offer to become the Assistant Golf Pro at Rancho Santa Fe back in southern California. During his Navy years, he continued to play on the golf team and did so well that an old Navy buddy encouraged him to leave school and take the job. Golf was where his heart and talent were and he had a family to take care of.

In 1949 my mother and father were on the road again. His job in California had ended abruptly when he wasn't promoted to Head Pro as quickly as he thought he should be. While back in San Angelo, they stopped by to see Lucille Perry, mom's life long friend from her school days. Mother and Dad stopped to see her at her small apartment. Dad pulled Lucille aside to ask her a favor. He explained that he was leaving on a "business" trip and asked Lucille if she would allow my mother and me to stay with her a while until he returned in a few weeks. Lucille replied, *"Sure, Curly, but you have to understand that I don't have any money. I have two kids to take care of, no husband, and my job just doesn't pay enough."* Curly replied, *"Oh, don't you worry darlin, I'll send you some money just as soon as I can."* So it was that mother and I moved in with Lucille, her son Brad, age seven, and Connie age three. Lucille was a struggling young divorcee trying to make ends meet. *"I didn't have a clue as to what was really going on,"* my mother would later tell me. He left her that day with the now famous words, "I'm going to '*hit-em* on down the road' and I'll be back before you know it". In his typical non-communicative and secretive way, he didn't tell anybody where he was going.

I'm sure the girls must have had fun when they were thrown together. Lucille told me the story years later that they turned off the electricity at the small apartment she was renting because they couldn't pay the electric bill. The neighbor across the hall let them "borrow" some electricity for the month until she got paid. Mother and Lucille heard about an "old boy" that had a place on the edge of town. He arranged to trade Lucille and Norma rent in exchange for feeding his horse. The two girls could be found early in the morning feeding the horse dressed for work in proper business suits, nylons and high heels shoes. Lucille was working as a buyer for a department store and mother worked as a secretary in downtown San Angelo.

Well, the story goes that my mother and Lucille were having a lot of fun reliving old times but things were soon going to change. By now, my mother was seven-eight months pregnant with my brother Lee. Lucille explained to Norma that she could no longer support us especially with another little one on the way. My father, scoundrel that he was, had left us there in San Angelo for months. Of course, he had not sent us any money as promised. So, my mother and I packed our meager possessions up and boarded a bus for Phoenix, Arizona. My father did arrange for us to stay with his mother Rosa, now remarried. Her husband owned a small row of bungalow apartments in Phoenix. After the war, housing was very hard to come by and they had all the bungalows rented.

2

"Mama! The Bus Is Leaving!"

So it was later in the summer of 1949 that we left San Angelo on a greyhound bus headed for Phoenix. We had traveled a good distance and it was late at night when the bus driver made a short ten-minute roadside stop. My mother being pregnant got off the bus to use the toilet. I got off the bus with her and was outside waiting when I saw the bus leaving without us. "Mama! The bus driver is leaving without us". I cried out to her as she was walking out the door. The memory of that starry moonlit evening has stayed with me all these years. We waited all night, abandoned, my mother and I alone on a cold bench until the next bus came through the following day.

When we arrived in Phoenix, it was in the heat of summer. We had no money, my mother was eight months pregnant, and grandmother Rosa was also struggling financially during those post war years. She had to give us an apartment that she could have rented-and she was none too happy about it. My father had put his mother and us into a very difficult place. Rosa was feeding and housing us every day when a letter came from my father. My grandmother opened the letter, even though it was addressed to my mother. The letter contained only a money order for fifty dollars, no letter. Rosa took the money enclosed as payment for food and back rent. Mother did not have a penny to her name. She was devastated and naturally very upset. My mother then called my great uncle Isom (older brother to Rosa) for help. Isom also had some apartments at the edge of town. So, we packed up again and moved to a small one-room bungalow. It was there that my little brother Carter Lee was born in the middle of all that confusion and disappointment. What a way for my brother to come into the world. Soon, my father showed up without a word. He didn't say where he was for almost nine months; he just said, "I had some business to take care of." We were off again, this time back to California. By now, my mother was having real doubts about her young hero, the charming guy from the wrong side of the tracks. But what could she do with two children to take care of all alone in the world? She couldn't go back home to mama.

My father, charmer that he was, continued to come up with stories to smooth things over. I suppose that love is eternally hopeful. A year later my little brother Bobby was born on September 15, 1950, exactly one year to the day from the birth of Lee. During the next several years, Dad became a gifted golf instructor and earned a place on the PGA golfers tour from 1952-54. He got his first opportunity as PGA Golf Pro at a small golf club in Calexico, California from 1953-1955.

In the summer of 1955 he was offered a much better position

as pro at the new Flying Hills Golf and Country Club back in the San Diego area. Here was a chance to finally move up the ladder. This was an ideal place to raise his family. With a wife and now a growing family of three young boys, it was a place with the promise of a better future. Perhaps there was a way to bring his double life to an end. But even then, the contradictions wouldn't go away. By day he was the charming and successful golf pro, but by night he was running crooked gin rummy games or gambling for high stakes. And we didn't have a clue.

His hopes and dreams were soon dashed. Flying Hills Golf Course suffered a major setback when San Diego real estate developers Charles du Pont and Stephen Fletcher both inexperienced at building a golf course made the tragic mistake of planting the wrong kind of grass. When the course opened in February the grass turned brown and died during the unusual cold snap in the winter of 1956. The golf course was forced to close and would not reopen for another year.

The catastrophic failure at Flying Hills Golf Club was Curly's moment of truth- his greatest test of character. He was $10,000 in debt and payment was required to open the golf shop (a lot of money in 1956). So, with no job and no immediate prospects, and through no fault of his own, he was facing the biggest failure of his life. Something snapped. He packed up his wife and kids and dropped them off at grandma's house (my mother's mother) now living in San Diego. His only words to us were, "I'm going away for a while to find work". That confusing summer day in 1956 changed my life and everyone around me. I would not see my father again for seven years until my senior year at Las Vegas High School in 1963. He had done his famous disappearing act, gone for the most formative period of my life. We were fortunate that grandma's doors were open. But her warnings to my mother, "I told you so, but you didn't listen", hung in the air without a word being said.

My first encounter with church and faith was completely negative. I was not searching for God but a neighbor kid, Jerry Butler asked me to join in Vacation Bible School at Scott Memorial Baptist Church near my grandmother's home on Texas Street in San Diego. I had never been to church so I was completely neutral on the subject. It was the summer of 1956. He described the crafts projects we would work on together, a chance to make new friends, and free cookies and punch. Everything seemed to go nicely until the very end when the teacher said that everyone should bow their heads for a prayer as we concluded VBS. I reluctantly bowed my head. I had no idea what to expect. "Now anyone who would like to be saved, please raise your hand to receive the Lord", she said. I peaked through my folded arms, moving my head from side to side while I was looking at the other kids. "These people must be crazy, saved from what?" I thought. The teacher had no idea the term "saved" was completely foreign to me. At ten years old, I didn't have the slightest idea what she was talking about. This experience taught me at a very young age that I didn't want anything to do with the "crazy people" at church. That experience stayed with me all these years.

Looking back now, I am thankful for the important time we spent with my grandmother Florence, great-grandmother Carrie, and great-aunt Hazel there in San Diego. My mother worked at a medical clinic near downtown. She was paid forty dollars per week minimum wage in the mid-fifties. My grandmother worked in a department store part-time for even less. My aunt Hazel worked for the U.S. Navy as a secretary for minimum wages as well. Great grandmother Carrie was seventy-five and getting up in age. She stayed home to care for us boys when we would come home after school. We got by, but barely. I soon realized that I needed to work after school to help the family make ends meet. I found a newspaper route that earned me enough to buy clothes for school, shoes and extras of all kinds that every boy needs. I thought about my dad a lot. When was he coming back? Maybe what my grandma said was true. "He's a no count! He's irresponsible, he doesn't love you". I was carrying too much of dad's baggage into my present and future but I didn't know how to get rid of it.

Even now the knowledge of my father's comings and goings after the summer of 1956 until April 1959 are sketchy. I had many conversations with dad after we reconnected in December of 1963. He told of his life of crime. From newspaper headlines, personal interviews, audio recordings I made about his life, I have reconstructed those law-breaking years until his death in 1983. This is the back-story of my father, a story that completely changed my life and brought me to search for my real father, my Heavenly Father.

While my dad successfully led a double life as a golf pro/professional gambler in California for many years, from 1956 forward his life was completely dedicated to chasing the golden ring as a full-time professional gambler. When he left us in the summer of '56 he headed straight out for Hot Springs, Arkansas-organized crime's provincial capital. This little town was a hot bed of illegal activity. Dad told me about the underground illegal "carpet joints" or gambling roadhouses that were discreetly tucked away and kept safe and protected through bribed officials. Dad started off there earning his living and gaining a reputation in backroom poker games and his favorite gin rummy. There he perfected his skills as a craps dealer, a twenty-one dealer and the like. As he later recounted, *"I was learning my trade"*.

I later found out that the well-known gangster Myer Lansky ran Hot Springs in large part. "The Springs" as it was known, had long been a favorite hangout resort of celebrity gangsters of the day going all the way back to the '20s with the likes of Al Capone. Hot Springs continued to flourish well into the '50s and '60s with gangsters like Lansky, Lucky Luciano, Costello, Mo Dalitz, Trafficante, and Marcello to mention a few. They were big players in a nationwide network of organized crime. Dad was well known by many of them.

The main source of Dad's daily bread was high stakes golf. He was a professional golf hustler and "rounder" as they called them. He moved in and out of places where he was not known. He posed as a frustrated doctor needing a vacation and re-laxation after the daily pressures of his medical practice. A little bet now and then made everything more interesting. Pretending to play golf poorly, porting a horrible golf swing and lacking understanding about the rules of golf he set the stage. "I let the "sucker" think he would easily beat me so we could raise the stakes even higher. Dad would loose the first five or six holes, then; on the back nine he would start winning, finish-ing with a dramatic "lucky" win. "It worked like a charm- they never knew what *hit em*". Dad would walk away with $500 to $1000 each game.

Along the way, the gambling roadhouses in Hot Springs, Corpus

Christi, Clovis, Reno and Las Vegas would become his favorite hangouts. They were the connecting points where dad was to meet the men who would later form his gang of seven for the heist of the Krupp Diamond.

3

The Krupp Diamond Heist

"We suspect many people share our yearning for more inside information about this crime and the pursuit of the criminals. Surely at some future date, the retelling of this crime story on television or in the movies will provide excellent entertainment."

"That Diamond Robbery."
Ogden Standard-Examiner June 24, 1959.

On April 10, 1959, three men—my father, Marion Carter Bowman, William Sneed Davie, and James George Reves— forced their way into the secluded Las Vegas ranch house of Mrs. Vera Krupp, tied her up, ransacked the house, and walked away with a small Minox camera, several hundred dollars in cash, and a flawless, 33.19-carat, Asscher-cut diamond ring, which they literally ripped from Mrs. Krupp's finger. Known from that moment forward as "The Krupp Diamond," the ring was believed to be a gift from Vera's ex-husband, Alfried Krupp.

He was the notorious Nazi war criminal who made a fortune supplying Hitler's army with weapons during WWII using slave labor from concentration camps—a crime for which he was later tried and convicted at Nuremberg.

"I gave up everything for her."- December 1958. A recently jilted Lou Manchon was taking out his frustrations on the golf course with his old gambling buddy (and professional hustler) Curly Bowman. As the two made their way across the back nine, Lou told Curly about the German munitions heiress he'd been having an affair with for the past three years. He described how she bought into a cash-strapped hotel on the Strip, made Lou president of the whole operation, and then, after getting dragged into bankruptcy court, bailed on him *and* the hotel. But that was not the worst of it. Lou also told Curly that somehow, news of their affair leaked back to Lou's wife, who immediately filed for divorce, calling Vera "a wicked seducer, [who] unlawfully, and willfully lured her husband away." "She ruined me," Lou seethed. "I gave up everything for her, and now she does *this* to me!"

My dad had never seen his friend this upset, he later told me. By the time they hit the 16th fairway, Lou was on a tear and divulged to Curly all manner of personal information that Vera shared with him in bed one night, the financial dealings of her estranged husband back in Germany—including large sums of cash he had been filtering into the US through secret bank accounts in Mexico—accounts Vera had access to. But it's what Lou said next that really made Curly's ears prick up. Apparently, Vera had a safe in the bedroom of her Las Vegas ranch house where she kept her own secret stash of mad money from Alfried's accounts. Judging by the renovations she'd made to the ranch, the second home she had in Bel Air, and the expensive jewelry she was always wearing, Lou figured Vera was hiding a small fortune in that safe. As the two began the long walk back to the clubhouse, a still fuming Lou said to Curly, "If you're ever looking for an easy take down check out that ranch."

"The Sparkler" - As was often the case with Curly, one afternoon out on the links had the potential to change everything. If what Lou said was true, Vera's secret safe could be just the score he needed to turn his luck—and life— around. So, Curly drove down to Mexico, traded his golf slacks and cleats in for some Levis, a pair of cowboy boots, and a nice Stetson, and headed out to the ranch to check out Lou's story for himself. In the four years since Vera's estranged husband bought her the Bar Nothing Ranch, she had converted the sprawling 518-acre property into a fully operational cattle ranch complete with a large herd of hybrid white-faced Brahma/Herefords. She renamed it Spring Mountain Ranch and made significant modifications to the existing ranch house, adding a guesthouse, a separate three-bedroom residence, bunkhouse, and a large swimming pool. Perhaps the most intriguing addition however, was a small guest bedroom that is connected to Vera's bedroom via a secret passageway hidden in the back of her wardrobe. Like most of the renovations, the room was built by Vera's live-in handyman/lover, Lou Manchon, who took up residence in the room shortly after the two began their affair. The inside of the house was filled with priceless antiques, first edition books, and exquisite European artwork she acquired during her travels abroad. None of these things mattered, however, to the burly, bearded gentleman in the newly-purchased Stetson standing in Vera's doorway, asking about boarding some horses. His attention was focused squarely on the massive diamond

perched on Vera's finger. "*I saw that big sparkler on her finger,*" Curly later told me, "*and that was good enough for me.*" Curly was convinced Lou was telling the truth. Somewhere in that house, Vera was hiding the lioness's share of the Krupp fortune.

"The Plan" – After leaving the ranch, Curly set to work formulating a plan. His first call was to John William Hagenson, a fence out of Hot Springs, Arkansas, who assured Curly that he had a contact in Miami who would take the diamond off their hands for $300K. He then made three more calls—one to Ed Hay, an expert safe cracker out of Dallas, one to fellow cat burglar James Reves in Hot Springs, Arkansas, and one to Bill Davie, a petty thief who was currently running a whorehouse with his wife in Ogden, Utah. Curly told all three to meet him in Las Vegas at the Traveler's Motel. Several days later, Curly, Davie, and Reves met at the hotel (Hay being delayed by a sick wife) and Curly filled them in on the ranch, the diamond, and the hidden safe. That night, they drove out to the ranch to scope out the area and talk through the logistics of the heist. Once Hay arrived, the four took turns staking out the ranch and learning the comings and goings of all of the ranch hands and Mrs. Krupp herself. They monitored the ranch for a full week, during which time, Hay was called back to Texas to take care of his still-ailing wife. Finally, on April 10th, after determining that Mrs. Krupp was alone at the ranch house, Curly and his gang were ready to make their move.

"Wired" – Curly, Davie and Reves went back to the Traveler's Motel to gather their tools. While there, Curly put in one last phone call to Hagenson in Miami to double-check on the fence. To Curly's dismay, Hagenson told him the fence—who was facing heat from the FBI for smuggling Cuban nationals out of

Havana— had changed his mind. *"If only I'd have just followed up by telling everyone to start packing their suitcases and go home,"* Dad would later lament. Before Curly could call off the dogs, however, Hagenson called back and told him the fence was back in. Tragedy averted, the guys checked out of the motel and drove out to the airport where they hotwired a car to use for the heist. After ditching Reves' car in a ravine a few miles down the road, they took the stolen car up to the ranch. Reves and Davie then waited in the car while Curly went up to the house to see if the munitions heiress was home.

"Don't pull anything and don't run for the police" - Inside the ranch house, Vera was enjoying an after dinner drink with one of her ranch hands (and current love interest) Harold Brotherson, when she heard a knock at the door. When she answered the door, she was approached by a man (Curly) claiming to work for the Acme Construction Company, asking if she would be interested in having the dirt road to her ranch paved. While they were talking, two men wearing handkerchiefs over their faces—one of whom was brandishing a gun— burst through the back door, yelling at Vera and Harold to lie down. "First, I thought it was a joke," reported Krupp. "Then, I saw he had a gun pointing at me, so I did lie down." Once they were on the floor, one of the men (Davie) ripped the ring from Vera's finger, leaving a small cut. He then hog-tied Vera and Harold together, gagged and handcuffed Brotherson, and covered their eyes with strapping tape. The men proceeded to ransack the house, taking roughly $700 in cash, a small Minox camera, and a Smith & Wesson pistol from Vera's purse. Despite their best efforts, however, they were unable to locate the safe. Exasperated, the men departed in a hurry. As they left, one of the men (Reves) told Vera, "When we go, you will hear two shots fired. Don't

pull anything and don't run for the police." Seconds later, the sound of screeching tires could be heard leaving the ranch, followed by two lone gunshots, then silence.

"The Escape" – Safely away from the ranch, Curly, Davie and Reves argued over what all three considered to be a failed heist. Not only were they unable to locate Vera's safe, but also in their rush to leave, they accidentally left behind a bag full of jewelry worth an estimated $200K they had found in Vera's bedroom. Curly, in particular, was livid. *"I never really cared about that diamond—that was always secondary,"* he later told me. *"What I really wanted was the cash and gold in that safe. That was the big score."* After locating Reves' car in the ravine, they drove to the airport, dropped off the stolen car, and returned to the motel to pick up their things. On their way out of town, Curly asked Davie where the ring was, and he told him he hid it in the gas tank of Reves' car. What Curly didn't know, however, was that the ring was actually in Davie's pocket, an insurance policy to ensure that Curly—who was still fuming over not being able to find the safe— didn't move forward on the deal without them. The three men divvied up the $700 in cash and split up, agreeing to meet in Miami in five days, where Hagenson's fence was waiting to take the diamond off their hands.

"We have been robbed!" – Meanwhile, back at the ranch, Vera managed to wrangle herself free. Unfortunately, she was unable to unlock Harold's handcuffs. After surveying the damage, the two made their way on foot to the foreman's quarters to get help. "He [the foreman] also thought it was a joke," said Vera. "I said, we have been robbed and held up," and finally he came out and looked and realized it was true." By this time, Brotherson's

hands had swelled up and begun to turn black and blue, so the foreman got a hacksaw and sawed through the links, though the cuffs themselves remained locked. Because there was no phone at the ranch, Vera and Harold drove out to the airport where Vera "called a friend and told them to contact the insurance company and tell them what had happened."

"Like all dumb thieves" – As Curly boarded a flight south to Miami, Davie and Reves drove north to Ogden, Utah, to pick up their wives. Along the way, Davie confided to Reves that he still had the diamond he told Curly he'd stashed in the gas tank. Later, on their way down to Florida, Reves gave his wife the camera they stole, and the two women took turns trying on the diamond ring. When the couples arrived in Miami, Curly was livid. *"Come to find out Jim and Bill had picked up their old ladies—like all dumb thieves will do— and told them, 'look here what a big deal we've done'. All of us guys are thieves. This is how we make our living. When we come into places, we don't all gang up and tell stories. We come in with different names; we meet at drive-ins, hotels, what have you. There's no way these sort of things should be brought out in the open, cause anytime you get over two people involved, well… let's just say, that if they didn't have snitches, nine cases out of ten, the FBI couldn't trace an elephant in about six foot of snow if he was bleeding from all four feet."*

By now, news of the "Krupp Diamond" robbery was all over the papers. Even worse, because of the diamond's value (and the diamond was believed to have crossed state lines), the FBI had gotten involved and was offering a $25,000 reward for any information leading to the diamond's recovery. Not coincidentally, Hagenson's fence got cold feet, and backed out of the deal again, leaving Curly and his gang with a now-famous diamond and no buyer. Realizing his dream score was quickly turning into a nightmare, Curly began planning the gang's next move. They needed another fence. And they needed one fast. As things continued to heat up in Miami, the next morning—diamond in hand—Hagenson and Reves boarded a plane to Chicago.

4

The Chase

"The Green Watermelon" – While Hagenson and Reves were in Chicago trying to unload the diamond, Curly stayed behind in Miami to keep an eye on the wives, who were spending money—and attracting attention— all over town. After two days of silence, Curly received a call from Hagenson, and the news was not good. Between the newspaper coverage of the robbery and the FBI poking around looking for leads, there wasn't a fence in Chicago willing to come within ten miles of the diamond. "We started calling it the Green Watermelon," my dad would later tell me, "cause that's about how much it was worth without a fence." Making matters worse, they'd now been on the road for over a week with nowhere near the bankroll they expected to be traveling with, and thanks to the wives' recent spending spree, they were almost out of cash. As Curly's temper began to flare, Reves assured him he had one last trick up his sleeve—a fence by the name of Red Holt thought he might be able to find a buyer in St. Louis.

"*Breaking up the set*" – After checking into the Chase Park Plaza Hotel in downtown St. Louis, Reves and Hagenson met up with Red, who took them to see Jason Kawin, a local jeweler who had been known to dabble in stolen merchandize. Unfortunately, as soon as they produced the diamond, Kawin produced a newspaper featuring a photo of Mrs. Krupp wearing the ring. Desperate for cash, Hagenson and Reves persuaded Kawin to take the diamond baguettes off their hands. They then returned to the hotel, pried the center stone out of its setting, flushed the platinum band down the toilet, and promptly left town. The only member of Curly's gang to catch a break that week, Hagenson was offered a job at a casino he used to work at in Havana, so he called his wife in Miami and told her to meet him in nearby Bossier City, Louisiana. Anxious to get out of town themselves, the Davie's and the Reves' agreed to drive her there. Curly—having had his fill of his friends' wives—made arrangements to meet them there a few days later. Unbeknownst to all of them, they were about to walk into a hornet's nest.

"*Here's where we all goofed up*" – By all accounts, Bossier City was the perfect place to lay low for a while. A hotbed of gambling, prostitution, and criminal activity, Curly figured they'd blend right in. And for the first few days, they did. Still low on cash, Reves and his wife headed back to Chicago to meet with another fence. "*Here's where we all goofed up*," dad would later confess. "*For some unknown reason, we all checked into the same motel. Well, there's a lot of gambling in that town, and it turns out someone got killed or something. So the police see a bunch of strangers all together in this one hotel with Nevada and California plates, and they just loop-scooped every one of us.*"

But Dad wasn't the only one to slip up. While running background checks, the police discovered there was a warrant out on Hagenson in conjunction with another robbery out West. So, instead of going to Havana, Hagenson spent the next month in the Bossier City Jail waiting to be extradited to California to stand trial. With Hagenson in jail, their mug shots out on the wire, and Curly's name now in the FBI's notebook, Bowman and Davie decided to make a break for the Mexican border.

"All he had to do was keep his mouth shut" – Meanwhile, Reves met with an old acquaintance named Joseph Simonetti, who told him about a fence in New Jersey named Berger, who might be willing to take the diamond. Because Reves and Berger had never met, Simonetti took a dollar bill out of his pocket, tore it in half and handed it to Reves along with Berger's phone number. He told Reves that he was going to airmail the other half to Berger so the two would be able to identify each other. Reves and his wife then drove to New Jersey, where, on May 22, they checked into the Cadillac Motel, just outside of Newark. Reves and Berger met, and upon matching up their dollar bills, Reves gave the diamond to Berger to show to the prospective buyer. The good news was that the buyer was interested.

The bad news was he wanted to have the ring appraised to make sure it was authentic. So, Berger took it to a jeweler and gave him Reves' name and contact info at the hotel. The jeweler, recognizing the diamond from the newspapers, called the FBI to claim his reward. The next morning, FBI agents, led by Robert Tagg, burst into the Reves' hotel room, and conducted a thorough search for the diamond. Eventually, an agent by the name of Bert Stickler found the diamond sewn into the lining of a sport coat, and Reves and his wife were placed under arrest. During his interrogation, Tagg struck a deal with Reves. "You give us all the facts, and we'll let your old lady off scot fee." Desperate to keep his wife out of trouble, Reves caved and told Tagg the entire plan from start to finish. "*All they would have had to do was keep their mouths shut,*" Curly would later complain to me, "*but no, you've got to have some dummy in the crowd who's stuck on some broad and he spills his guts.*" After forcing Reves to sign a written confession, Tagg locked him up, released his wife, and sent out a nation-wide APB on my dad, Davie, Hagenson and Hay.

"I didn't want to go down without a fight" – The next day, Curly picked up the morning paper. *"There's my dummy partner and his old lady on the front page."* So he and Davie decided to drive down to Tampico, Mexico to pick up some phony passports, and head to Brazil. Before leaving Texas, Curly bought a brand new 1959 Ford Thunderbird convertible with bright red upholstery—not the brightest move for two guys trying not to attract attention. "*I might as well have pulled off all my clothes, set my hair on fire and run down the road naked,*" he later told me. After picking up their passports, Curly arranged to sell the car in Mexico City to—of all people—the president of Mexico's nephew. While sitting at the airport waiting for the kid to pick up the car, a Mexican police officer that had been tipped off to Curly and Davie's whereabouts took both men into custody. "*I thought, well I'm a sonofabitch,*" Curly later mused. "*They had the airport completely surrounded with the Federales. Come to find out we were on the FBI's Most Wanted List.*" After being interrogated at the station, Curly and Davie were handcuffed and loaded into the backseat of a police car. "*The Federales took us half way across the bridge in Laredo, where the FBI were supposed to meet us. Well, when those two Federales got out of the car, I pushed the*

front seat over with my foot, crawled out, and leapt over the bridge into the water. I knew they would capture me," he told me. "I just didn't want to go down without a fight".

"The End of the Line" — Curly was quickly re-apprehended, and he and Davie were both handed over to the FBI. The next day, they were arraigned in Laredo, Texas, with bail being set at $25K each one. With Hagenson still awaiting extradition in Bossier, Reves in custody up in New Jersey, and nobody else to call for bail money, Curly and Davie remained in county lock-up for a month and a half. Finally, a U.S. Marshall arrived to take the two men to Las Vegas to stand trial.

Dad was convicted and was ordered to serve 10 years and pay a $10,000 fine. During his travel from Washington State to Las Vegas, the (unnamed) U.S. Marshal assigned to guard/accompany prisoner Bowman made a startling announcement while they were sitting together in the back seat of the vehicle. The Marshal looked at my dad with a twinkle in his eye: "Hey Curly, I've got something to tell you. You won't believe this- we found the safe you were looking for in Vera's bedroom. We discovered it behind a secret sliding panel in the closet of her bedroom." My father later said to me, "Jimmy, that just blew me away. I sat there boiling and fuming inside. I knew he was telling me this just to aggravate me, but what could I do; it was all over now".

Bowman Family: Upper Left to Right, Curly Bowman, wife Norma and boys Lee, Jim, Bob, Lower Right Jim with Dad in 1956, Curly in 1978

Top: Jesus Film Premier showing in 1984 during traditional Tarahumara Easter Ceremonies

Below: Jim with a Church Planting team from Northern India

Mixtex Believers in Manzanito

Tarahumara little girl

Believer struggles to read

Zapotec Woman with cat

5

The Auction of a Lifetime

Fast-forward to December 1963. Supreme Court Justice William O. Douglas in a surprise move, ordered my dad's release from McNeil Island Federal Penitentiary on his own recognizance in order to appeal his case to the 9th Circuit Court of Appeals, asserting he was denied his constitutional right to appeal his conviction of the theft of the Krupp Diamond. He traveled by bus to Las Vegas, Nevada to the home of my mother- now re-married. My two brothers and I were ironically living in Las Vegas. When he arrived at the door, I was home alone sick with a bad cold. I answered the door and there stood my father who had been gone for eight years. I looked straight into his eyes; Curly smiled and said: "Hello Jimmy, I've come home". I stood there shocked, and amazed, and couldn't believe what I'd seen. My mouth dropped to the floor. Struggling for what to say, I didn't know if I wanted to hug him or tell him to go to hell. Sarcastically I said, "Last time I saw you, you said you were just going to the grocery store to buy milk and bread. What happened? Where the hell have you been for all this time?" He told me he'd been in prison- serving ten years for stealing the Krupp Diamond. I had known nothing about this and was stunned and amazed. I couldn't believe that my father, who I idolized all these years, was telling me that he was guilty of such a crime.

We talked for hours while my mother was at work and my brothers were at school. He told me that he had rented a room at the Lee Motel and as soon as I was well enough to come visit him. He left before the others came back home. I sat there wondering what to tell my mother and brothers. This was a pivotal moment for the family and me.

I reluctantly reconciled my relationship with my father but not without doubts that lingered. "Is he just using me as his get out of jail card? What's his angle?" Doubts persisted, but in the end, love won over doubts and fears. I loved my father, even if he was using me. The longing I had to be with my father was finally fulfilled. With the blessing of my mother, I left home to go to live with my dad at the Lee Motel in Las Vegas. I completed high school and started my freshman year at UNLV. During this time my dad and I stayed up late every night while he shared the entire story of the Krupp Diamond caper with me in full detail. We eventually worked together to develop and present his case to the 9th Circuit Court of Appeals. We had no money, but we convinced Las Vegas attorney Harry Claiborne and his paralegal Annette Quintana to help us with the appeal. Claiborne later became a U.S. Senator from Nevada.

With some help from the paralegal, I stayed up late many nights preparing the case to go before the 9th Circuit Court of Appeals in San Francisco. It seemed that dad was trying to get out of prison on a technicality. He claimed the court erred in ruling a claim of privilege of self-incrimination and that he, Davie and Reves were forced to testify against each other and were thereby denied their 5th Amendment rights. I remember so vividly the day that we walked into that huge courtroom just me and dad, and the three justices who were present to hear the case. The sun was shining through the windows sending streaks of light onto the floor below. In what seemed like a cathedral of law and justice the final word came down. On October 12, 1965 the three justices denied the appeal and my dad was sent back to prison to serve out his sentence. He served another three years and was released in 1968. Our time together off and on in 1964 before he returned to prison was formative for me. It shaped me in ways I only recognized much later.

Before their respective captures, this rag-tag band of thieves had led federal agents on a wild, cross-country chase punctuated by an unforgettable cast of characters, car chases, and assorted capers—including my father's ill-fated attempt to escape the Mexican *Federales* by leaping off a bridge into the Rio Grande while handcuffed. As stated before, all three men would eventually stand trial and be sent to prison (and one of their accomplices would be killed by gunfire). As for the diamond... following Vera's death in 1967, the legendary stone would make headlines once again when Richard Burton purchased the ring at auction for a record-breaking $305,000 as a gift for his wife, Elizabeth Taylor.

I've never thought of my jewelry as trophies. I'm here to take care of it and to love it, for we are only temporary custodians of beauty."

—*Elizabeth Taylor*

Fast-forward to December 12, 2011 at Christie's Auction House, New York City. Nine months after Elizabeth Taylor's death, hundreds of fans, friends, celebrities, jewelers, dealers, and collectors flocked to Christie's flagship saleroom at 20 Rockefeller Center to take part in the largest, and most highly anticipated estate auction of all time. Comprised of one thousand one hundred and seventy eight different lots, the Elizabeth Taylor Collection drew bidders from thirty-six different countries, participating in person, online, and over the phone, all vying for a piece of Hollywood history. In true Elizabeth Taylor fashion, the auction began fifteen minutes late. The room was packed. The excitement was palpable. One lot at a time, each item in the glossy five-volume catalog exceeded its estimated value by leaps and bounds.

The magnificent Tajo Mahan Diamond given to Taylor by Burton on her 40th birthday, sold for $8.8 million—more than eight million more than the original estimate, and the famous Le Peregrina Pearl necklace Burton gave her in 1969 sold for an astounding $11.8 million—more than *nine* million more than the original estimate. Auctioneer Francois Curiel later joked, "We arrived at the estimates without taking into account the Elizabeth Taylor premium." Curiel further commented, "This is the only time in my career that I've seen people bidding so ferociously, jumping from $2 million to $4 million in one bid." Though there were many spectacular pieces up for bid that evening, it was Lot #80—the Elizabeth Taylor Diamond, formerly known as "The Krupp Diamond" that generated the most excitement.

The bidding began at $2 million. Within 30 seconds, it had reached $5 million. The room was so quiet, you could have heard a pin drop. The only voice was that of the auctioneer, steadily raising the bid in increments of two to three hundred throusand at a time, his eyes darting back and forth between the front row and the bank of agents taking bids via telephone in the back of the room. When the bidding stalled ever so briefly at $7.4 million, he leaned forward against the podium and egged on the three remaining contenders, imploring, "It's the Elizabeth Taylor Diamond. She wore it every day." As if on cue, a paddle went up raising the bid to $7.5 million, then $7.6. Seconds later, the hammer dropped on a final bid of $7.8 million. The lucky winner was Daniel Pang, a South Korean businessman who was bidding on behalf of E-land World. As Pang sat back in his seat, a contented grin spreading across his face, the room erupted into thunderous applause—a fitting end to a truly spectacular story. Or is it?

6

A Changing World

"Father, talk to me!" It was 1963 and I wanted to know all the
details. From the moment dad sat down to tell me the story of
the Krupp Diamond everything had changed. From Vera Krupp
to the shocking story of my father's involvement with the diamond I was shaken to the very core. At the time it seemed like
a story filled with excitement and lots of drama. But as time
went by, the story affected my sense of who I was: ...the son of
a thief. Was my dad a hero or a villain? The truth is I was humiliated, embarrassed, and ashamed. For many years, I was afraid to
tell anyone about it. I was too young to understand why I felt
so humiliated. I wanted to crawl under a rock, just be invisible.
I had longed for my father to be in my life and now it was such
a let down, it left me so empty. I had to make a choice, would I
follow in my father's footsteps, or would I take a different path.

I didn't know at the time how much my dad's story impacted
my life... in very negative ways. We lost the case and dad was
to face imprisonment once again, this time to serve out his

sentence. I was devastated, disoriented, and I made some decisions I would regret later. I got married too young without really knowing what I was getting into. I failed to really think about best choices for my future. The cultural shifts in our country swept me up in the late 1960s. The winds of change were blowing like a hurricane. Things in the American culture were changing at a speed not known by anyone before in history.

In 1966 I was studying at UNLV, married with a child on the way, working full time at the Las Vegas Sun Newspaper. I was employed by a well-known man in Vegas, Hank Greenspan who was famous for making good with his Jewish brothers by running guns from Miami to Israel during the Jewish fight for Independence and Israeli statehood. He was now a famous publisher that everyone admired for his stands for justice.

As I mentioned, the nation was in the midst of volcanic change. In the headlines of the newspapers all around the country people read:"US sent 500,000 troops to Vietnam". Many of my friends were being drafted into the Army; others were going to Canada. I was fortunate to receive a medical waiver. The cultural revolution, the explosion of violent crime, the rise in the precipitous use of drugs, widespread rebellion against authority and the traditional family, and the sharp turning away from God were clear markers that things were changing in a big way. It was a time of race riots in black communities, the founding of the Black Panthers. Even the Beatles were changing from the innocence of, "I Want to Hold Your Hand" to the cynicism of "Nowhere Man". The words kept ringing in my head.

"He's a real nowhere man, sitting in his nowhere land,

Making all his nowhere plans for nobody.
Doesn't have a point of view, knows not where he's going.
Isn't he a bit like you and me?
Nowhere man, please listen.
You don't know what you missing.
Nowhere man, the world is at your command."

The Beatles were holding their final concert tour as a group in the U.S.A. In a March 1966 Maureen Cleave interview with John Lennon he said that the Beatles were "more popular than Jesus". He explained, "Christianity will go. It will vanish and shrink. I needn't argue about it; I'm right and I'll be proved right. We're more popular than Jesus now; I don't know which will go first- rock 'n' roll or Christianity. Jesus was all right but his disciples were thick and ordinary. It's them twisting it that ruins it for me." Later at press conferences Lennon explained himself. He stated that he was only commenting on the decline among churchgoers. That was controversial but it got me thinking. Who was this Jesus? I'd heard of him but I didn't really know anything about him. I tucked the question away and didn't think about it again for a long time.

People all around me were having discussions about God and spirituality; it was part of the national conversation. Most of us did not know what it meant to be spiritual, not really. The cover page of TIME magazine of April 8, 1966 said in big bold letters; "GOD IS DEAD?" The article went on to say "The Enlightenment had killed the possibility of belief in God. The death of God, meaning the Christian God who existed at one point, has ceased to exist". It was a provocative thought, but I brushed it aside. Since my life was not affected by these claims,

I ignored it. So many other things were changing that I couldn't keep up with it all.

In 1966 Anti-War protesters were marching all over the country, burning their draft-cards. The National Organization of Women (NOW) was launched. The Irish Republican Army (IRA) was waging a civil war. China's Cultural Revolution had begun. Joan Baez and one hundred and twenty-three anti-draft protesters were arrested. Revolution was in the air-ever everywhere. What was happening? Who was right? Who was wrong? These were questions of conscience and moral strength. I wanted answers, but I didn't know how to begin to find them. What did it really mean to have moral character? I, like most people did nothing.

"Nowhere Man" was wearing a hole in my soul in the spring of 1966. It was a stone in my shoe. The pain kept coming back. I didn't have a real direction for my life that was satisfying. I was that nowhere man. The words rang out in my head *"Nowhere Man please listen. You don't know what you're missing. Nowhere Man, the world is at your command"*. "What command?" not mine. Everything was out of control. What did the Beatles know about me? It was just another silly Beatles song. But the message still swirled around in my head. Yup, one thing was certain, I was that nowhere man.

I was preoccupied with the failures of my dad's life; everything seemed fuzzy and unclear. I didn't want to feel anything, I just tried to ignore it, but I couldn't. Maybe I was obsessed with an absentee dad, I don't really know. My father had been absent for the most formative period of my life. There had been only silence. I could remember his absence from all the little league baseball games I played in and Boy Scout events when every other dad was there, except mine. I remember when all the other boys went to a campout with their fathers. Where was my dad? I didn't have a dad. "He died when I was little," I would tell other boys. I was always standing there very sad and alone. I had become a loner; I pushed people away for fear they would get too close. From the time my father left my mother and us boys at grandma's in San Diego, I went to the mail box nearly every day for years hoping that a letter would come... not so much as a birthday card. There was only silence. "Nothing, nada, zip. Suck it up kid! He disappeared for good. Get over it; your dad isn't coming back". The words kept going through my mind.

Through so many years of my childhood my true feelings were of loss and abandonment. It was like that stone in my shoe was never going away. I felt like a failure, but why? I didn't do anything. I'm no psychologist, but it seemed to me that I was all twisted up inside, I was angry, irritated, confused and rebellious and I didn't even know why. I seemed to be going through the motions of life without purpose and direction. I wasn't like other boys and girls. Everyone had a father, but where was mine? I resented what my grandmother always said about my dad. Yet, it was true. My dad was a no-count. He lived only for himself. Though grateful for their sacrifice I resented being raised by my mother, grandmother, and great grandmother, with no dad around. The questions remained. Why was I here? Did I really matter? There was pain and a void inside. How do you heal the heartache when your father is missing? I just stuffed it down deep inside. By the mid 60's my childhood pain still affected my life.

Songs have always spoken to me, to my inner person. 1966

there was another song that had a tremendous effect on me, Burt Bacharach and Hal David's song:

What's it all about, Alfie?
Is it just for the moment we live?
What's it all about when you sort it out, Alfie?
Are we meant to take more than we give
Or are we meant to be kind?
And if only fools are kind, Alfie
Then I guess it is wise to be cruel
And if life belongs only to the strong, Alfie
What will you lend on an old golden rule?
As sure as I believe there's a heaven above, Alfie
I know there's something much more,
Something even non-believers can believe in
I believe in love, Alfie
Without true love we just exist, Alfie
Until you find the love you've missed you're nothing, Alfie
When you walk let your heart lead the way
And you'll find love any day, Alfie
Alfie

It was a high impact song for me with lines that raised many questions: "Is it just for the moment we live? Are we meant to take more than we give, or are we meant to be kind? If life belongs only to the strong what will you lend me on an old golden rule? The strong, the weak, a golden rule? There was something inside that was longing for answers, but where would I ever find them? Did life belong to the strong? Was there a heaven above? Did I believe it? I thought and thought but no answers were in sight. Again, the words to another hit song were speaking to me. I turned to the words of Simon and Garfunkel.

Hello darkness, my old friend
I've come to talk with you again
Because a vision softly creeping
Left its seeds while I was sleeping
And the vision that was planted in my brain
Still remains
Within the sound of silence

Now, that's a song I could get into: the sound of silence. Darkness was my friend, silent, cold, and damp. Yup, that was me! That was something that made sense. Or did it? Being numb to life, is that how I wanted to live? Would I go and join the revolution? Which one would I join? What did they really believe? Did I believe the same as they did? These questions needed answers NOW. Pop culture and music were the symbols young people cared about but as a country, we had lost our way; we were on the Eve of Destruction. This message was being played on every radio station in America.

The eastern world, it is explodin',
Violence flarin', bullets loadin',
You're old enough to kill but not for votin',
You don't believe in war, but what's that gun you're totin',
And even the Jordan river has bodies floatin',
But you tell me over and over and over again my friend,
Ah, you don't believe we're on the eve of destruction.

I was angry. I was frustrated but where could I go for clarity? I needed someone to guide me. I needed a straight path, with straight answers, something that would provide encouragement, comfort. I needed the guidance of a father but he wasn't there. I was fatherless. I felt completely alone, and the voice of my father was silent. I couldn't go on like this. Out of all the different directions to go, I again asked myself which Revolution I should join?

7

Looking for Answers

Fast-forward to 1970. Life seemed to be on automatic pilot. I was still living in Las Vegas. Life all around me was filled with the world's temptations. Drugs, Sex and Rock 'n' Roll were everywhere but fortunately I had taken a different path. I was married to Maureen and we now had two children. As a couple, we liked to listen to Joan Baez and read about David Harris a prominent anti-war protester who was eventually imprisoned for draft resistance. Joan first caught my attention when she appeared onstage at Woodstock in 1969. I heard her sing while I was in college. I first read about Joan Baez and David Harris as articles were appearing in the LA Free Press, a counter-culture newspaper that was making headlines at the time. They were appealing primarily because of Joan's beautiful voice and commitment to pacifism and anti-war activities. I learned later that her family had converted to Quakerism and she had con-tinued to identify with that tradition. Joan's non-violent ideals appealed to me. War was not the answer. Joan Baez along with Judy Collins, Emmylou Harris, Joni Mitchell and Bonnie Raitt were popular at our house along with a wide variety of rock bands that were coming on the scene. The anti-war and revolutionary tone resonated with me. This was a revolution!

There were also some other voices speaking to me in the early 1970's. *Jesus Christ Superstar and Godspell* were making a big impact. They started out as Broadway plays and movies and became very popular. The cast was clothed as hippy flower children. Both productions were somewhat controversial, but overall they were another voice speaking into the culture about the person of Jesus Christ, just another voice out of many. I thought, "There are many paths to God, this Jesus is just one more." I remember a song people were humming called "Day by Day".

Day by day
Day by day
Oh, Dear Lord
Three things I pray
To see thee more clearly
Love thee more dearly
Follow thee more nearly
Day by day, Oh, Day by day
Day by day

By the summer of 1970 things took a turn for my family and me. I was working for KORK-TV, the local NBC affiliate selling time at the station and making local TV commercials. It was a good job and paid well. I was offered a job in Tucson, Arizona at the station there. My marriage was going through some rough spots and a move seemed right to me. Maybe it would help. I did well at the new station, and while I was there I met

Ken Byrnes (not the famous one) in 1971. He was making TV commercials too. Through a long list of circumstances, he offered me a partnership in his company Aztec Film Productions. During that time, I started to travel back and forth between Phoenix and Tucson, Arizona a great deal. Most of our clients were in Phoenix because it was growing and had become headquarters for many national corporations that needed TV commercials and product films. The job was lucrative and somewhat rewarding, influencing people to buy products and services. That felt good. I was changing the world for the better. At least I told myself that I was making the world a better place. It seemed like everybody wanted to change the world, but was my way the right way? At least I wasn't doing anything dishonest. But deep inside I didn't believe in what I was doing. Something was missing.

I was away from home for long periods and my job became so demanding that problems soon surfaced. Maureen had taken second or even third place in my life. Conflicts over being an absentee father became more intense. Sound familiar? I was following in the footsteps of my own father. I wasn't willing to put my wife and children first. I loved the kids, but I didn't know how to balance home life with my professional life. They deserved more than I was giving them. Quality time spent with my wife and children was foreign to me. But, there was something inside me that said I needed to re-prioritize my life; in fact Maureen was demanding it. What I needed was a complete overhaul.

In the summer of 1973, after a long search, I sold my share in Aztec Films and took a job in Phoenix with Young and Rubicam West. With headquarters in New York, it was a Madison

Avenue ad agency looking to establish a foothold in Phoenix. At the time and even today it is one of the world's largest consumer advertising agencies. Coming in contact with a group of high-powered creative people that were running things had a profound effect me. I was coming home to Tucson weekends temporarily until I got settled in. I learned a great deal about how the "big boys/girls" did things. I was very impressed with myself. I was assigned to work as a "broadcast producer" in charge of everything from TV commercials to documentary films for commercial purposes. At twenty-seven years old I was doing what I loved to do. It felt like I was important, that I had a bright future. Or did I? I jumped from the frying pan into the fire.

I thought it would be better for me and my family to live in Phoenix because I would not be traveling long distances so much and it would enable me to spend much more time at home. It was time to arrange to make the move. It was January of '74 when I drove Maureen and the kids to Phoenix to look at houses and to talk about what a plan of transition might look like. But ultimately we decided to leave the girls in school and not move until after they were out of school at the end of the school year in late May.

Meanwhile, I continued to rent a room and come home weekends. But, staying in Phoenix was difficult and lonely. I was fine during the daytime but after work and nighttime I went stir crazy. One weekend, I was in a bookstore and found a copy of "Autobiography of a Yogi" by Paramahansa Yogananda. The inside cover drew me in. "Yogananda is a man whose inspiration has been reverently received in all corners of the globe... There is something inexpressibly beautiful in the spiritual teaching which comes out of the East. It is able to heal and change the soul of the West. It is the teaching of Self-Realization." *Riders Review, London.* What's more, in the front of the book was written, *"Except ye see signs and wonders, ye will not believe"*- John 4:48. This was interesting and at the same time puzzling. I expected to hear a Yogi quote from the Hindu scriptures, but to hear him quote the Bible inexplicably drew me in. Paramahansa seemed to be a welcoming influence in my life. My mother was an early proponent of New Age religion back in the late 40's and 50's. There was always a book or two on reincarnation in the house. These books stressed a "higher power" and "secret wisdom" that could be found by a few special people. She was fascinated with Eastern ideas that were not popular when I was young. Most of my friends were nominal Christians so I was embarrassed to talk about reincarnation with them but in the mid-sixties it seemed more "hip", especially appealing in pop culture. Still my mother influenced my early spiritual life more than I knew. The New Age thinking in her day was called New Thought Movement. As an adult I had rejected her influence but now my mother's influence seemed to take hold in me again. This was the "Age of Aquarius", associated with harmony, love, understanding, sympathy and trust. These concepts were part of the lyrics of the day, like in the 1967 smash-hit musical Hair, with its opening song Aquarius, by a musical group called the 5th Dimension. Maureen and I saw the musical in Vegas when we were living there. The song opened with the lines:

> When the moon is in the seventh house
> And Jupiter aligns with Mars
> Then peace will guide the planets
> And love will steer the stars
> This is the dawning of the Age of Aquarius

I thought that Paramahansa might know something about the Age of Aquarius and the promise that it brought. I bought his book and read it cover to cover learning about an organization he founded called Self-Realization Fellowship. I read that he came to the United States as a missionary from India many years earlier. A famous quote caught my attention: "Let my soul smile through my heart and my heart smile through my eyes, that I may scatter rich smiles in sad hearts." He claimed the powers of insight. "By the practice of meditation, you will find that you are carrying within your heart a portable paradise." This portable paradise sounded good to me. But, one verse above all really captured my attention: "The light of the body is the eye, if therefore thine eye be single, thy whole body shall be full of light" (Matt 6:22). I was taught at SRF that Hindu's placed a red dot on their foreheads as a symbol of this truth. Paramahansa claimed he was an "ascended master" because of what he taught. That is, he claimed the same status as Jesus. I wanted to explore this more, and oddly the Bible was a source of the real truth.

I was taking in everything Paramahansa taught. I signed up for a correspondence course. I read the first lesson, filled out written answers to the questions that appeared at the conclusion of the lesson. Then I would send it back for the next lesson. His teachings and assertions were that all religions eventually lead to the same god. This mantra is still being heard today. He again and again quoted often from the Bhagavad Gita the ancient Hindu scriptures but was equally comfortable quoting from the Bible: John 1:1-3 "In the beginning was the Word, and the Word was with God, and the Word was God...All things were made by him (the Word or Aum to Hindus); without him was not any thing made that was made." He was an expert and practitioner on the subject of Kriya Yoga. For example, he said in his book: "Kriya Yoga is twice referred to by the Lord Krishna", India's greatest prophet- in the Bhagavad Gita. One stanza read: "Offering the inhaling breath into the exhaling breath and offering the exhaling breath into the inhaling breath, the yogi neutralizes both breaths; thus he releases *prana* (life force) from the heart that brings life force under his control." The interpretation is: "The yogi arrests decay in the body by securing an additional supply of *prana* (life force) through quieting the action of the lungs and heart, he also arrests mutations of growth in the body by control of *apana* (eliminating current). Thus neutralizing decay of growth, the yogi learns life-force control."

This was a remarkable claim: "the yogi learns life-force control"? In other words the yogi could learn the power of life and death. Wow! I wondered whether if this was true. I was fascinated by his assertions and continued to read and study about Kriya Yoga. I was spending more and more time at the Self-Realization Fellowship (SRF) branch in Phoenix.

As I said before, he often quoted the new Bible verses throughout his book and teachings. They were new to me anyhow. For example he said: "Jesus came, not to destroy the law and the prophets but to fulfill them. When questioned as to the greatest commandment, he replied: ...thou shalt love the Lord thy God with all thy heart, and with all thy soul, and with thy entire mind, and with all thy strength". (Mark 12:30) Then Paramahansa added "To love God with this completeness is possible only through union with God, a state that can be attained by yoga meditation wherein one realizes the truth of Christ's words: *The kingdom of God is within you" (Luke 17:21).* This was attractive but at the same time confusing. It sounded good, but I still had many questions and remained skeptical. Something inside me that I couldn't understand or explain cautioned me. I felt apprehensive about what seemed like a false promise of "secret wisdom" and "ascended masters" that could be found waiting just around the corner. Deep inside me I felt a warning to go very slow. After a year of study at SRF I had yet to find what I was looking for. The point was that I was searching and I was hungry for truth. Where was the promise of inner peace and tranquility to be found in this Age of Aquarius? I didn't know it at the time, but Paramahansa was tempting me into believing in a false messiah, a false Jesus. The teaching seemed to be about Jesus, but I didn't recognize His voice. My skepticism continued to grow and it led me to want more of the truth found in the Bible. I wanted the true Jesus, but where could I find him?

A branch of SRF had been established in Phoenix by his follow-ers. It was a beautiful all white building on Central Boulevard. It looked like a small version of the *Taj Majal*. It was situated on several acres of land with peaceful gardens and a lake complete with swimming swans gliding gracefully. I often went to eat my lunch there. It was a wonderful tranquil place to get away from all the "noise and clamor" of a life so full of activity. I missed my family, but the SRF was a place to hide out, looking for peaceful feelings though at times I found peace illusive.

Often I would go to SRF to partake in their evening services after work. It was fashioned after church services in the U.S. As you came in however, there was not a stick of furniture though there was wall-to-wall carpeting throughout. On the altar in front was only a large protrait of Paramahamsa Yogananda, and photos of his guru Swami Sri Yukteswas Giri and also Jesus placed prominently. Seeing Jesus made me feel somehow at peace with myself, it felt good. But, on the other hand what stood out to me was Paramahansa who was already dead. He died in 1952 in Los Angeles living only to be 59 years old. So, his claim to have control over the life force created more suspicion in my mind. One night I was seated dressed in my fancy and expensive silk-suit and tie. I felt suddenly out of place. At the front of the sanctuary were three young men who were converts singing songs in Hindi. These men were similar to what we called the *Hari Krishna* people who wore ochre-colored tunics and shaved their heads. They were all over America at this time, made popular by the Beatles when they embraced Ravi Shankar as a great man of God. Ravi's music during this era was being played everywhere. Even the Beatles were saying that there were many paths to God, and Hinduism was the best one. John Lennon's words, "We are more popular than Jesus" came back to me. "Jesus is alright, but his disciples were thick and ordinary. It's them twisting it that ruins it for me." Thick and ordinary? I was getting more and more confused. There were too many voices inside of me.

8

The Day That Changed My Life

During one particular evening I got off work and entered the main sanctuary of SRF. I took off my shoes (as was the custom) and sat cross-legged with my arms extended on my knees. I was saying my *"Aums"* the incantation that was to calm one's spirit and give peace and joy. It was a daily ritual that I performed. While I was settling into this position, I heard a voice behind me saying, "What you are looking for you will not find here". I looked behind me to see who would be saying such a thing. There was no one, just an empty wall. I was perplexed and wondered where the voice came from. But, deep down inside the words I heard had a profound impact on me. I was already beginning to doubt the claims of Paramahansa. The claims of Kriya Yoga and secret knowledge were fading. A moment of decision was clear, I looked up front and I saw the Hari Krishna people. I thought to myself "I am not a Hindu, and I don't think I could ever become a Hindu; the only thing I learned from him (Paramahansa) was his constant mention of Jesus." I needed to learn more about Jesus, but where could I go? I was strangely drawn to Jesus. Who did I know who could tell me about Jesus?" I slowly got up and scooted out the door. I got into my car and when I turned the key to the ignition, the radio came on announcing, "Tonight, Billy Graham is at A.S.U. stadium". I said to myself, "That's it, that guy knows all about Jesus!" I looked at my watch. It was 6:30 PM leaving just enough time to get there. It was May 10, 1974. I will never forget it as long as I live.

I drove to the stadium in Tempe, and saw the big crowds and I looked at the people. I felt out of place. Suddenly, it seemed like I didn't belong there. Everyone seemed to fit the common stereotypes of church people - the "establishment." In my mind they were all losers, and in my arrogance I wondered how could they know the truth. I was struggling with two paths, one that seemed to discern between right and wrong, good and evil, the voice of my conscience. I had heard its voice before. But another voice from within was leading me toward Paramahansa. Which voice would I listen to? The stronger voice influenced me toward the claims from the Bible.

From a counter culture perspective I should have been against everything these people stood for. They were the source of everything I thought was wrong about America. They were FOR the war in Vietnam, or so I was told. I marched against that war. These people were foreign, odd, out of place. I said to myself "What am I doing here?" But these were moral questions, right and wrong issues. I was being pulled in two directions. My struggle was bigger than the Vietnam War; it was about the war within? Could I be honest with myself? I wanted to turn back and just say forget it. It made no sense to continue, but something inside was saying, "Just be patient, wait for Billy".

The church choirs were beginning to sing the old hymns of the church like "Rock of Ages" and it was an offence to me. I can't say why, it just was. It seemed like Billy Graham took forever to reach the podium. I didn't understand the world of the Christians- they made no sense. There it was again, that inner voice pulling me in the other direction.

Sherwood Wirt later wrote in the August 1974 issue of Decision magazine:

> "Everything about the Crusade was seemingly touched by a gracious hand. The evenings were warm and balmy; the crowds were responsive; the music superb; the workers had a mind to work; the preaching was relevant and Spirit-filled. A power beyond man was evidently at work in the hearts and the throngs nearly filled the stadium night after night. What was once Zane Grey and Wyatt Earp country was now holy ground. The Fiesta Bowl became a bowlful of love, peace and joy."

I was touched by the fact that Apache, Pima, Navajo, Hopi, Yavapai, Mohawk and many other tribes were present. On that night in May, Native American evangelist Tom Claus of the Mohawk tribe presented Billy Graham with an eagle headdress and plaque with the name "Natani" which means "Warrior of the Great Spirit". It was not until years later that these events resonated with me since Native people would play such a big role in my life.

That night, God was doing something in me that was inexplicable and even miraculous. The reason I sat there that night was Jesus. I didn't know much about Him but Billy Graham knew all about Jesus. I wanted to hear Billy from start to finish. I cannot remember much about what Billy preached except one thing that stood out. Jesus' very own words impacted me: *"I am the way and truth and the life. No one comes to the father except through me." John 14:6* The words hit like a ton of bricks on my head and heart. Those words stood out in direct contrast to everything I heard from Paramahansa. That was it! That was why I was there that night. Jesus is THE WAY; no one comes to our heavenly father except through Him. I needed my sins forgiven, and God had made a way. I thought it was so amazing. God knew we could not do it on our own. He loved us so much that he was willing to pay the full price for my sin. We had all been blinded by sin. Everything made sense now. The claims of Paramahansa and the Beatles faded away. The Holy Spirit was there that night, and I asked Jesus into my heart, and that bowl full of love, peace and joy was coming out to greet me. I felt God's presence for the first time and I cried like a baby. Coming down from the stadium and onto the field where Billy Graham stood, I went forward that night to surrender my life to Christ. Walking down the stadium onto the field was symbolic to me. I thought I was so high and mighty, but going down voluntarily was brought low and it felt good and right. I believed for the first time that Jesus had risen from the dead and that changed everything. It was a supernatural experience that has stayed with me for over forty-five years. It was the day that changed my life forever.

On that balmy night in May, I gave my whole heart to Christ and the first thing he said to me as I stood praying, "You are now a soldier in the army of the Lord!" "Who me? A soldier?" I thought I must have been hearing things. "I'm not a soldier, remember Lord… I'm the non-violent one, a war-protester. I can't become what you are asking, oh no." The thoughts kept flashing through my mind and then I heard another voice again. "I want you to quit your job, go back to Tucson, sit at my feet and learn of Me. "Oh no, what will Maureen say?" Was I just hearing things, was I crazy out of my mind, just confused and tired? "That's it, I'm tired, and it's late".

I called Maureen to tell her everything that had happened. It was late that night when I found a pay phone near the stadium. There were no cell phones in those days. I called her and she was alarmed that I was calling so late. She thought that something had happened. The first thing I said to her was: "You'll never guess where I've been." I said it with great anticipation in my voice. "Ok, I give up where have you been?" she asked. "I've been to a Billy Graham crusade, and guess what? I got saved!" I said it boldly and with conviction. There was a long pause at the other end of the phone. "You did what?" I might as well have said I had run over a dog or something. "You did what? I can't believe what you are saying". I came right back to her with, "That's not all, God told me to quit my job, go back to Tucson, sit at Jesus' feet, and learn about Him." Another long pause, "Ahh! Right, sure, I think you'd better come home and we'll talk about it." When I hung up the phone, I could tell that she was not pleased. But, my mind was clear and I would do just what the voice from the Holy Spirit was telling me to do.

That weekend, I went home as usual. We talked about my experience at the SRF that I heard a voice and it told me to look elsewhere to find what I was looking for. I told her all about the miraculous events that took place that night. Then she said the most amazing and unexpected thing " Well, now that you mention Jesus, there is a woman across the street that keeps coming over here and talking about Jesus constantly. She won't shut up. I can't get rid of her." Her name was Shirley and she came over to the house the next day and we listened to her talk about Jesus in a way that was new to me. She talked as though she personally knew Jesus. She claimed she was walking and talking with Him every day. She said if I would seek Him, I would find him. "Return to me" God says, "and I will return to you". She was quoting Zechariah 1:3. I didn't know that people quoted directly from the Bible every day. I didn't know that Jesus was interested in me personally. No one had ever talked to me like that. I was amazed. "I can talk to Jesus and he actually hears me?"

I wanted to know all about this Jesus that talks to other people too. I wasn't the only one hearing from God. If it were true, it was the most fantastic discovery of my life. But, was it true? I was not raised to read the Bible or to look to it for guidance. That weekend Shirley invited us to Grace Chapel, a church on the other side of Tucson. It was far from us, but if it offered all the things she said, it would be worth it. We arrived that Sunday in May of '74 to a very unique experience. People were raising their hands and loudly praising the Lord. The singing was contagious, filled with joy and thanksgiving. I was overwhelmed with a peace in my soul that I had never experienced. Could it be possible that I was experiencing what I had longed for all my life? What's more, the church was filled with counter culture people or "Jesus People" as they were called at the time. I found a group of people who I could relate to and I was indeed experiencing intimacy with God. "Come near to God and he will come near to you". It seemed like the purpose of my life was made clear to me that day. For the first time I knew why I was created. He had a purpose for my life. The Holy Spirit was a new form of communication from God and it was washing over me. I didn't understand all of what was happening to me, but I understood that God was talking to me and I wanted to listen to everything He had to say. He was a father to me, a real father. No more silence, no more deception. God was honest and true; I had joined the Jesus revolution. God had offered me a peace treaty signed in the blood of Jesus Christ his son. Now I had access to God through faith in his son Jesus, access by this grace in which I stood that day and every day since.

I went back to Phoenix that night pondering everything I had heard and saw that day. I turned in my resignation at Y&R and headed back to Tucson without a job, but I had clarity and direction for the first time in my life. I jumped into my new experience with God and the Holy Spirit, looking to Him for direction. Now I knew what it meant to be called a "Jesus Freak". It was a term frequently used of those who followed Jesus. It was a demeaning term that I was now proud to claim for my own. I remembered vividly what he said to me that fateful day at the Billy Graham Crusade, "You are now a soldier in the army of the Lord". Those words kept ringing in my ears. I did not know what that meant exactly. A calm peaceful voice within was speaking, confirming all these things I had experienced that weekend. It was the voice of the Holy Spirit. I would follow him and He would show me the next steps. The Holy Spirit was speaking to me about quitting. "Ok, I quit my job" I said. "I'm now ready to sit at your feet and learn, Jesus!" I said it with my whole heart. Whatever the cost, I was ready to pay it. No holding back, this is want I wanted. I was baptized two weeks later to publicly proclaim my newfound faith in Jesus. My experience that day would be summed up in the words sung by Keith Green in his great ballad:

Until Your Love Broke Through

Like a foolish dreamer, trying to build a highway to the sky
All my hopes would come tumbling down,
and I never knew just why
Until today, when you pulled away the clouds that hung like
curtains on my eyes
Well I've been blind all these wasted years
and I thought I was so wise
But then you took me by surprise
Like waking up from the longest dream, how real it seemed
Until your love broke through
I've been lost in a fantasy, that blinded me
Until your love broke through
All my life I've been searching for that crazy missing part
And with one touch,
you just rolled away the stone that held my heart
And now I see that the answer was as easy,
as just asking you in
And I am so sure I could never doubt your gentle touch again
It's like the power of the wind
Like waking up from the longest dream, how real it seemed
Until your love broke through
I've been lost in a fantasy, that blinded me
Until your love, until your love, broke through

At last I had found my father, my real father, my heavenly father, a good father. He would bring each day the love and acceptance that I so desperately needed. He was a father that would talk to me and I could talk to Him. He rolled away the stone that held my heart. It was like the song says, it was like waking up from the longest dream, and I was lost in a fantasy that blinded me, until His love broke through.

From the summer of '74 though the summer of '76 I accomplished just what I had hoped to, I sat at the feet of Jesus and learned of him. I also took a job at the Arizona Star and Tucson Citizen advertising department. It was a stable job and I had time to devote to my family, the Word and prayer. The job earned enough to send my two girls Tami and Kim to Christian School at Grace Chapel. My attention was on the Lord and how He was directing my life. I didn't have all the answers about Christian living, but I wanted to give my children the opportunity that I didn't have to grow up knowing about Jesus. Everyday, during lunch or any spare time available I read the Bible with great enthusiasm and interest. Day and night, it didn't matter, I read from cover to cover this new "Word of God" that held my interest and challenged me along the way. While reading the Bible, I had the most overwhelming sense of my own pride and previously unrecognized sinfulness that was heavily weighing on my heart and mind.

I also learned that God was on record speaking to men through His Word and through the Holy Spirit, as He did when I first came to know him. I read in Exodus 33:11, "Now God spoke to Moses as a man speaks with his friend". The Lord spoke to Adam, to Noah, to David and many, many more. My own experience was the same. I was having spiritual dreams and visions that I knew were coming from the Holy Spirit that guided me. His words weren't just for just special holy men of God; they were for me and for everyone. This amazing fact held my attention from that first day until the present. I would need the guidance that I received to carry me through the dark days ahead.

9

Devastating News

In the summer of 1976 just as Maureen and I were beginning to learn how to live this new Christian life, tragedy struck. Maureen wanted a divorce. She had found someone else, and was not happy living a life with someone who "talks with God" and who is called a "Jesus freak". She couldn't live with someone who was constantly going to church and was seemingly obsessed with the Bible. Even though she went to church with me, she was not convinced about Jesus. "We no longer had anything in common", she said. She had tried it and did not want the Christian life. What's more, three months after I moved out she was diagnosed with stage four-breast cancer. This metastatic type of breast cancer was what the doctor called an "undifferentiated carcinoma". This meant that the tumor did not form a hard mass. It formed a jelly like mass that was almost indiscernible. It had moved to her lymph nodes and was rapidly spreading all over her body. She didn't even know until it was too late. It was very aggressive, and needless to say I was devastated, confused, and downright angry with God. Everyone was giving me advise about what to do. All I could do was pray and ask God for a miracle. He knew the way. I needed to trust him even if everything around me was crashing down around my head.

Again, someone very close to me was suddenly taken away. It was beyond my control. Where did I go wrong? Was it my fault? Did God do this? Was He testing me, or did He have a plan that I knew nothing about? I struggled with this for many months. I prayed, and prayed. Meanwhile, doctors had not given Maureen much hope. She did agree to have mastectomy and a second surgery in an effort to save her life. Miraculously, the surgeries did help her temporarily, and they gave her a few extra years of life. The sad news was that during the crisis I kept hoping the she would change her mind and we could get back together, though it was not meant to be. She seemed recovered at first but a few years after she was remarried and she and the girls had moved to Bullhead City, Arizona to be near her mother and close family members she passed away from metastasized cancer. Happily she had turned to the Lord and walked with him before her death. I would miss my girls very much. They too were being taken from me. It seemed like my world collapsed and everyone I loved was gone.

It seemed like it all happened so fast. I struggled to get my balance, I was again feeling like a Nowhere Man. Where are you God? Where is the love I once felt so strongly? Have you abandoned me? I tried to pray but it was no use. He was not listening, or so it seemed. Suddenly, I was passing through a time of great testing of my faith. I began to doubt my experiences with the Lord. "God did not speak to you", the devil would say to me. The exclusive claims of Jesus were troubling me. I didn't have the words to respond to the voice inside me that was challenging everything I believed in. But then the Holy

Spirit said to me "Who is the Lord of your life?" It was equally troubling to my spirit when I read the words of Scripture
*"But, whoever disowns me before my Father, I will disown before
my Father in heaven" (Matt 10:33)*. These were solemn words
but clear words Jesus spoke to me. There was a huge struggle
going on inside; it seemed like I had to make a choice. Would I
serve the Lord or would I go back into the world? I reluctantly
chose to follow the Lord, but in a kind of lukewarm way. I just
muddled along in my pain and bewilderment wondering waiting for a better day, or worried if that day would ever come. I
was going to church, but my joy was gone.

Then overlapping these events early in 1976, I became involved
with a new national call to prayer and fasting. It was called the
"If My People" movement. It was organized around the nation's bi-centennial event coming up on July 4th. The nation was
to celebrate its two-hundredth birthday. The movement was
centered on II Chronicles 7:14 *"If my people, who are called by
my name, will humble themselves and pray and seek my face and
turn from their wicked ways, then I will hear from heaven, and I will
forgive their sin and will heal their land"*. I was one of those who
needed my sins forgiven, as I was still carrying the weight of the
failures of my life; the pride and arrogance of my sin weighed
heavy. There were several of us in the church who were committed to prayer and fasting, including me. The nation was going
through some hard times. The energy crisis, the cold war, dé-
tente, and inflation were weighing heavy on everyone in our
nation. A God given opportunity was before me to repent. The
4th of July fell on a Sunday. My job, with others throughout the
city was to mobilize the city to prayer and fasting on Friday the
2nd, Saturday the 3rd, and ending with a huge rally at the Tucson
Convention Center on Sunday the 4th.

Not only Tucson, but also cities across the nation were coming together as a way of showing unity and purpose. Churches, businesses, and individuals joined hands. On the 4th of July we were privileged to have *Second Chapter of Acts* present to sing the "Easter Song" to celebrate the risen Christ. The musical ensemble played a composition especially written for the event "If My People." It was all a huge success but more importantly it called my attention to God's sovereignty over the entire nation and also over me. "God is still in charge". Though this was a big boost to my faith, I couldn't shake these feelings of hurt and shame. "Oh God, deliver me from this trial," I cried out to God. I felt the weight of the world lift off my shoulders as I prayed. Little did I know HIS reign over my life would soon take on a positive new direction.

Earlier that year I met Jay Johnson at church. He was starting a new ministry called "Miracle House Ministries". It was a prison ministry to soon to be released federal prisoners. The prison system felt it was a good investment for those who needed help with housing, a job, and counseling prior to their release. They wanted to hire an outside organization that would keep an eye out for these prisoners and help them adjust to life on the outside. Jay bought an old, outdated motel near downtown Tucson and was in the middle of making the needed repairs. He needed volunteers to help get ready for the men who were coming out soon. Once the men arrived, during their time of transition, volunteers could befriend prisoners, learn of their basic needs and help them personally make the transition. Some were even ready to learn more about Jesus. It seemed like a good way to channel my personal problems into something positive for the Kingdom of God.

It was just the right thing for me. I could help prisoners make the transition because I had a father who had been in prison. Because of this, I felt I could befriend them and have some credibility with them to help through the hard times. I volunteered for that first year. After that, Jay asked me to be on the board of his fledgling young company. Miracle House contracted with the Federal Prisons to provide these services and since it was a new program, the rules had not been well established and monitored. As a board, we worked through many, many problems that face most young organizations. I learned many things about myself through this experience. I could see that God had gifted me with good common sense along with administrative skill. In addition, I had a heart for those who did not know about this loving, caring God. Someone had to tell them about a father who would love them, care for them, and who would protect them. Once again, God was preparing me for things to come. But, meanwhile I stayed with Miracle House until 1986 as a board member and volunteer.

Grace Chapel during the years 1974 to 1978 was a place of refuge and healing for me. A close friend called it a "Spiritual Camelot" experience. It was place where many of us experienced a powerful move of the Holy Spirit over a sustained period of time. This was a period of a great outpouring of God's Spirit that came to be called "The Jesus People Movement." It was during this time that many people began publicly confessing their sins or rededicating their lives to Jesus Christ. In this atmosphere, people were not only receiving Christ as their Savior, but were intensely moved by their own sinfulness and their complete and thorough need for God's mercy and forgiveness. I witnessed alter calls not only for salvation but also for sanctification, healing and deliverance. I heard a cappella singing in tongues. I met people who were giving their all to God. We were called "Holy Rollers" or other names that were meant to harm or make fun of us. I just ignored their taunts. What mattered is that I no longer felt fatherless; I no longer felt estranged culturally and socially.

I felt completely at one with Jesus and the people he called his own. I was healed of my wounds. Sometimes we believers would spend hours together worshiping the Lord in the Spirit and in song. Regularly members of the congregation would come forward with a word of prophesy, words of wisdom, and the Word of God proclaimed in new ways I had never experienced before. There were waves of healing that I felt over and over again during worship, week after week. At Grace Chapel, Jesus had truly orchestrated and authored a revival that I later learned was happening in many places throughout the USA.

The cultural transition was coming to me in new forms of gospel music. This cultural shift was felt in the larger secular community as well as in the Christian community. There were fresh new artists and a new sound started showing up on the gospel music charts. People like Keith Green, Chuck Girard, Phil Keaggy and Barry McGuire -who was famous for the song "Eve of Destruction"- all had experienced a powerful conversion. Barry McGuire and Phil Keaggy teamed up at a concert in Tucson. Matthew Ward and the Second Chapter of Acts and many others were singing songs that were meaningful.

God was healing my feelings of rejection and the pain and resentment of years not knowing my father. He was healing me of the shame and guilt I felt at not being able to save my marriage and the frustration of not understanding why God had not healed Maureen of cancer. Most of all, I still felt the emptiness of the loss of my children who were far away from me. Healing came slowly, but in the middle of all the pain and suffering, His presence was overwhelming. I felt immersed in an ocean of His love. It was totally a God thing, as the Holy Spirit filled me. "Lord Jesus, thank you for your healing touch."

In February of 1976 there was an earthquake in Guatemala. It was the most destructive earthquake in history measuring 7.5 and it caused over twenty-three thousand fatalities, and left seventy-six thousand injured. It was a disaster of mega proportions. While Guatemala often has earthquakes, never one as devastating as this one. Many thousands of people were homeless. When the Guatemalan earthquake happened, many at Grace Chapel were predisposed to helping their friends in Latin America, since it was a missionary church. Their enthusiasm touched me. I realized that the time had come to stop sitting on the bench. It was time to put my faith into action.

Grace Chapel was sending a group of men down to Guatemala to build two hundred simple houses in the aftermath. I was so enthusiastic about going. I tried to take off time from work, but reality soon set in. I realized that I was not ready for this; it was not God's time. I was so envious of those who did go, but I gave generously toward the project and we heard back from the team regularly. I wanted to participate in the action, but not just yet. It was very encouraging and satisfying to see the pictures the team brought back of the completed homes and happy faces of those who were fortunate to get a house. By this example, God was showing me what kindness and mercy looked like, how much His leadership through the church was something to be admired, something to emulate. I could see God's love and I understood it in real, concrete ways.

A missionary family working in Cuba and Mexico founded Grace Chapel. Dad Casteel, as he was called, was the patriarch and son John Casteel was the senior pastor. They were driven out of Cuba during the Revolution and had relocated to Mexico and they stayed for many years. Dad Casteel was older and supplied the newer church with lots of Godly wisdom. Although the family founded a church in Tucson, they maintained a strong connection with the churches they founded in Mexico and throughout Latin America. Dad Casteel would make regular trips to Mexico. He and John spoke fluent Spanish and it was a big encouragement to the believers in Mexico to have a church in the U.S. who prayed for them and who gave regularly. Dad and John would invite many Mexican pastors to Grace Chapel and they gave exciting progress reports. The Mexican pastors were truly an inspiration to me. They were another example of caring, loving people and I wanted to be like that too. I wanted to learn more about the believers of Mexico and find a way that I could imitate their faith. Perhaps now was time to put my faith into action. Something was drawing me to Mexico. It was exciting to me, but I really didn't know why, I just knew. God was answering my prayers.

10

First Trip to Mexico

After the earthquake in Guatemala, my interest in Mexico grew. I wanted to be a part of outreach there, but knew very little about it despite living in the border town of Calexico when I was a child. I asked Pastor John if he would let me go to Mexico sometime but he was reluctant to let me go. He patiently said, "Wait a while and I will see what I can do, maybe next time". Well, "next time" didn't come for a long time. I kept asking and asking, praying and praying. Finally, in March of 1979, more than two years later, I received an invitation from Pastor John's brother Richard to go with him and others to a Bible School in Durango, Mexico. They were having a conference of believers and they had invited Richard Casteel to be the main speaker. I was thrilled. I was going as the photographer for the event. Wow! I truly believed that God was answering my prayers. Maybe I had sounded like the persistent widow. I didn't care; I was on my way to Mexico.

When we reached Durango, we were assigned to stay in little

shacks that the students lived in. I quickly adjusted and became friends with Juan who could barely speak a few words of English. I spoke no Spanish at all, though the sounds and intonation of the language were familiar from childhood. Juan and I gestured and found simple ways to communicate. Together, we witnessed a baptism of forty to fifty new believers. We went to the river to take part in this exciting event. I took many photographs of everything from the baptism, to eating together in the main hall, to the church services at night. The baptized believers were full of joy, giving thanks for everything God was doing in their lives. It was an experience that stayed with me. God was providing me with experiences that would change my life and send me in a completely new direction.

It was about this time that I was attending young adult Friday night services at the Vineyard Christian Fellowship near the University of Arizona. I got to know Randy Reynolds who was pastoring the church. A friend who could see that I needed Christian counseling recommended him to me. I was still dealing with the same issues that I thought Jesus had healed me of the year before. I needed God's help to fully sanctify and restore me to emotional health. It seemed as though my complete healing was elusive. I didn't know it then, but I learned that God sometimes heals over time. Though I tried to hide it, it was apparent to everybody but me that I was still dealing with lingering issues of fully forgiving my father, Maureen, and others who had hurt me. It seemed like I had problems and issues that I couldn't shake. I began sessions of professional Christian counseling with Randy and I would often go on Friday night to hear him teach. He was not like other preachers. I could identify with him. He was very laid back and a "counter culture" guy like me. We seemed to hit it off, to bond.

Randy helped me through biblical relationship concepts I was previously unaware of. I learned about the importance of love and respect, of family, of grace-based relationships, conflict resolution, of limits and boundaries, and of anger management. He taught me the biblical role of a husband. But most importantly, Randy taught me how to apply these Godly principles to my daily life. So together, Randy and I worked on my personal situation and made specific applications to my past. But most of all, I felt like I could forgive my dad, Maureen, and even myself for so many failures of the past. My time with Randy led me to recognize that God provided the keys to unlock my inner man: *"My sacrifice, O God, is a broken spirit, a broken and contrite heart you, God, will not despise". (Psalm 51:17)*

At this time I was going part time to Grace Chapel, but I learned many things from Randy about *grace* at the Vineyard. As I have said earlier, I was not brought up in a Christian home that taught biblical principles. My mother has been an early proponent of New Age principles that were in opposition to God's principles. It was clear to me that I still had a long way to go to learn the basics. Randy opened up the whole realm of *grace-based relationships.* I learned first that grace comes from God. Common grace is God's goodness in the every day of life. God loved his children so much, that he sent his Son to die on the cross, so that whoever believes this message, has eternal life. (John 3:16) It was a message that I needed to hear over and over. It is God who loved us first when we were still filled with confusion, hate, distrust and rebellion. That was another miracle in my life. Keith Green's song came back to me again as I pondered everything that God had done in my life:

All my life I've been searching for that crazy missing part
And with one touch,
you just rolled away the stone that held my heart
And now I see that the answer was as easy,
as just asking you in
And I am so sure I could never doubt your gentle touch again
It's like the power of the wind…

I found comfort in knowing that grace creates safety and a sense of security. Grace creates peace, freedom, responsibility, and respect. For me the most important, was forgiveness. I read the Scripture, "God created everything that was created". It was through a relationship of grace he gave eternal life. The Scriptures spoke to me and to my inner man clearly, but slowly. With this grace comes the ability to love without fear. I now understood that we could live at peace even with the memory and pain of loving someone who is unloving, or unlovable. God opened up his words to me personally. I had the guidance I was longing for coming from my Heavenly Father. I had a remedy for fear now. The apostle John says, *"There is no fear in love. But perfect love drives out fear."* (I John 4:8) It meant so much to me that Jesus loves the fatherless, the poor, and weak, the orphan, the widow and the untouchable. He especially loves the underdog, and everybody in the world who will follow Him.

As a son left virtually fatherless by his earthly father, this spoke to me. I couldn't reject this message. Only love, God's love and grace, can transcend this broken world. Why hadn't I heard this before? Who would withhold this message of God? Who would be so unloving to keep it for themselves? I knew that God wanted His message to go out to the world, to be extended to the ends of the earth. Who would go to those who have never heard before? Jesus said: "*All authority in heaven and on earth has been given to me. Therefore, go and make disciples of all nations, baptizing them in the name of the Father, and of the Son, and the Holy Spirit, teaching them to obey everything I have commanded you. And surely I am with you always, to the very end of the age*". (Matthew 28:18-20). Now, that's Good News! That was a message that could provide purpose for a lifetime.

When I came back from Durango I was very excited to share my Mexico experiences with everyone who would listen. In May of 1979 Randy Reynolds asked if I would share my slides with the Friday night group. Though I didn't have any experience speaking to large groups, the Friday night audience seemed small enough that I wasn't intimidated. So, I spent lots of time getting the slides together, writing an informal script, and even rehearsing my presentation several times. I relived the experience of Mexico for my friends and listeners and I could tell by the many positive responses that I was connecting with the audience.

One person who spoke to me after the presentation was Carla Peterson. She wanted to know more about my experiences in Mexico. I told her that I had little or no ministry experience in Mexico, as this trip was my first. As we talked, I could tell there was something different about this girl. She asked the most astute questions about the people of Durango. She shared a little about herself. She had been studying at the University of Arizona and recently completed a Masters Degree in Spanish and Bilingual education. She was teaching elementary school at Mission View Elementary where many Yaqui Indian students attended from a nearby Yaqui *barrio* right in the heart of Tucson. I knew very little about the Yaquis, but as I talked to Carla it was clear that she knew a lot about them and I was drawn to her and to the Yaqui Indians. I was curious, and wanted to know more. She was happy to share and so we made a date for coffee. We connected immediately. Carla was so different from anyone I had previously known. We talked and talked about many things but the common theme was the Indigenous people of Mexico whom she was passionate about. Our first "date" was at the premier showing of the Jesus Film at El Con Theatre. The film would later become well known among Christian audiences. The following week, she invited me to attend the Yaqui Revival Center where she had become a regular attender. This became yet another amazing experience that would change my life. I had not known at the time, but step by step, God was on the verge of giving me a completely new purpose and a new direction in life. Carla and I bonded very quickly. My life took on new purpose and direction. The Holy Spirit was guiding me from that point on. I had another great "Aha" moment that shook my world for yet another time. I saw relationships in a new and important way...as relationships of trust. I could trust Carla with all that I had been through. It was the beginning of a beautiful relationship because it was grounded in the Scriptures and the Holy Spirit.

God gave us the gift of the written and spoken Scriptures to point the way. He also gave us the word of our own testimony to be his witnesses. How we were to use these tools was not clear yet, but I knew I was headed in the right direction through a reliable promise. These were the keys that unlocked hidden treasure. I knew that now because I had the help of the Holy Spirit. *"But the Advocate, the Holy Spirit, whom the Father will send in my name, will teach you all things and will remind you of everything I have said to you."* John 14:26 I found that the Holy Spirit guided Carla and me throughout our lifetime. HIS promises are reliable and true.

11

Trust, Rewards and Punishment

Meeting Carla and our close friendship were important events in my life. Jesus was teaching me to imitate Him in everything. "Be *imitators of God, therefore, as dearly loved children, live a life of love, just as Christ loved us and gave himself up for us as a fragrant offering and sacrifice to God." (Ephesians 5:1).* He also said in Ephesians *"husbands love your wives as Christ loved the church and gave himself for it".* That meant that I must imitate Christ in my marriage and everyday life. But, if there was no trust between God and myself, how could God possibly work in my relationship with Carla or anyone else? I learned that I must believe God who is worthy of trust. In a committed relationship trust is everything. God has earned our trust not "because he said so", (like my father often said to me), but because he demonstrated love through his example. That's how real love works. God showed me what a loving and good father does. This was another big step in forming healthy, Godly relationships especially with a spouse. I understood intellectually how God's view of marriage worked, but emotionally I still wasn't completely there.

God was demonstrating to me how much the Bible was written as a guide to everyday life. God is concerned about our welfare…simply because He loves us. It now guided my relationship with Carla, a relationship that was growing into more than a friendship. I didn't have to earn His love. It's in His nature to love. It's what makes God tick. He created us in His image and likeness. This helped me to open up to Carla and share the details of my life with transparency. The big question of God's love was now settled, but living it out in my everyday life was still a challenge. I trusted God to offer the kind of guidance I needed to lead me to the right helpmate for my life. But, would I get the love, trust, compassion, concern and affection I needed? What are the simple truths that lead us to practice this new kind of love…God's love? It would take me some time before I felt that I had mastery of a love that trusts God and others.

While I had this great "Aha" moment, I needed to work it out in everyday life. My relationships with my father, ex-wife, and children had confused me. I felt I had to earn their love…that I had to work for it. Certainly everyone in our society teaches us rewards and punishment at various levels. We are constantly jumping through hoops every day in our daily circumstances. We earn a degree from college, or we get a bonus at work for a job well done. Human love is naturally very selfish, self-centered, it's natural desire is "to get" more than it gives… remember the song Alfie? The words were enough. God's love conquers all, but in God's way. There is no compromise. That is the part that made me stumble. I still had more to learn through the power of the Holy Spirit.

We all remember the film "The Godfather". It has become very renowned because of its main character Don Vito Corleone (played by Marlon Brando) as the leader and *"Godfather"* of a fictional New York crime family. The movie begins with Johnny Fontane, a famous singer and Vito's godson, seeking Vito's help in securing a movie role; Vito dispatches his man, Tom Hagen to persuade studio head Jack Woltz to give Johnny the part. Woltz refuses until he wakes up in bed with the severed head of his prized stallion and racehorse. The plot is very simple but profound. Without a conscience or fear of the consequences, they all understood the language of a *Godfather*. The "Godfather" used inventive ways to rule and "lord it over" by fear and intimidation. This is an extreme example, but the "godfather" serves his master, the father of all lies and deception -the devil- and all his dark angles.

Bob Dylan said it best in his song *"You've Got to Serve Somebody"*

You may be a construction worker working on a home
You may be living in a mansion or you might live in a dome
You might own guns and you might even own tanks
You might be somebody's landlord, you might even own banks
But you're gonna have to serve somebody, yes
You're gonna have to serve somebody
Well, it may be the devil or it may be the Lord
But you're gonna have to serve somebody
You may be a preacher with your spiritual pride
You may be a city councilman taking bribes on the side
You may be workin' in a barbershop, you may know how to cut hair
You may be somebody's mistress, may be somebody's heir
But you're gonna have to serve somebody, yes

You're gonna have to serve somebody
Well, it may be the devil or it may be the Lord
But you're gonna have to serve somebody

Characters like Don Corleone may get away with "lording-it-over" people in a reign of terror and fear, but they too serve somebody- they serve the devil. As the song says, it may be the devil or it may be the Lord, but you're going to have to serve somebody. The Lord of Heaven, the creator of ALL things says that those who choose the devil will pay the wage of death forever. That was his warning to me.

God, our Heavenly Father will keep these promises of rewards and punishment both in this life and the life to come. God has made us with a moral compass that guides us along the way. We don't have to be taught murder is wrong, or lying, or stealing. No matter where you are from, what country, or what culture, that moral code is written on our hearts. We were created in God's image and likeness. This is perhaps the most important lesson I have learned; God created us all in his image and likeness. The Scripture says: "He has set eternity in the human heart". (Ecclesiastes 3:11) It is impossible for God to lie. My father will reward me but HE must be number one. God demands that I have no other gods but Him. If not, God has a clear warning for all of us. He created us with the right, the free will to choose between fear and hate or love. That God loves me has been demonstrated over and over again. Jesus says this in his teaching to the disciples: *John 15:9-11 "As the Father has loved me, so have I loved you. Now remain in my love. If you obey my commands, you will remain in my love, just as I have obeyed my Father's commands and remain in his love. I have told you this so that my joy may be in you and that your joy may be complete.*

Carla and I made a lifetime commitment to each other that year. It was a commitment that has had its ups and downs and its problems, but because we both were committed to serve God first, we have lived a life of service together for over forty years. It's only part of a great reward that is not yet fully revealed. Our obedience to Christ, while certainly not perfect, has guided and directed our way. Jesus gave us purpose and direction for our new life together.

12

Preparation Time

Carla and I were married in a simple ceremony at our new Tucson home on December 22, 1979. It was the eve of a new decade. I felt free to love and to be loved. While I had dealt with my past, my fatherlessness and failure of my first marriage, I now felt it was time to move on. I felt just like King David when he wrote the words of wisdom: *"Blessed is the one whose transgressions are forgiven, whose sins are covered. Blessed is the one whose sin the Lord will not count against them and in whose spirit is no deceit"*. (Psalm 32:1-2) The past was behind me, forgiven completely; a bright future was now ahead. I was free to commit because of Jesus. The wounds inflicted by my earthly father had been replaced by the unfailing love of my heavenly father.

The first thing in our courtship and marriage was to establish prayer in our new life together. Praying together was new for me but Jesus guided and directed me in this too. We continued to pray and earnestly seek God's direction in our lives. We prayed for our future, for our friends and family, and for those we would serve in the future. We also prayed for the believers in the Yaqui village. By this time we had both spent a lot of time among the people of the Yaqui village called "Old Pascua". The Yaquis called themselves "Yo'eme" meaning "people". These cross-cultural experiences over the next few years were a preparation for what was to come. God was placing on our hearts the needs, hopes and cry of native people.

The Yaquis described themselves as "the Easter People" as most had converted to Catholicism through Jesuit missionaries during the colonial period of Mexico where they were originally from. Carla and I became fascinated with the Easter Ceremonies held each year in Old Pascua. The Yaquis history was a story of a people longing to be free. During Mexico's struggle for independence from Spain, the Yaqui considered themselves an independent nation. When Mexico won their fight for independence, the Yaqui people refused to pay taxes to the newly installed government. An armed conflict started and became known as the "Yaqui Wars". There was a series of revolts. Since the Spanish first had contact with the Yaquis in 1565, they had a reputation of being fierce warriors and fighters. These wars continued through until the time of the Mexican Revolution in 1908 when at least five thousand Yaqui people had been sold into slavery. Many died of hunger without help, and begging for food. The Mexican government continued a policy of extermination and colonization. The Yaquis continued their fight until they were finally defeated.

In 1937 Mexico established a Department of Indian Affairs (INI), and the Yaquis received five hundred thousand *hectares* of land and restored citizenship. But during the Mexican Revolution in 1908, many Yaquis had fled the country to Arizona where eventually they established tribal headquarters and received formal recognition by the U.S. Government. The Yaquis settled in urban *barrios* including Old Pascua in Tucson, Barrio Libre, New Pascua, and Marana. Since learning a little of the history of the Yaqui people, Carla and I were interested in their syncretized Catholic Easter rituals. The Yaqui deer dancers were fascinating to watch. The Yaqui religion is a mixture of Christian and old Yaqui beliefs learned from the teachings of the Jesuit priests and missionaries. It relies on dancing, prayer, song, ritual, and drama. Very specific music is played when the dancers perform depending on whether their masks are on or off. As many as four or five dancers perform in unison or individually. The Yaquis believe that ritual or ceremony can access the spirit world and that dance eliminates the harm that has been done to them.

The longing to be free is fundamental to all peoples. I was deeply moved by the Yaqui's slavery, poverty, and affliction. The freedom we all have available in Christ was not clear to the Yaquis. I wanted to do something about that. People from all over Tucson (mostly Yaquis) always went to witness a dramatization of the Passion of Our Lord. Part of the drama team impersonated the evil men who persecuted Christ. The pursuit of Jesus, his capture, symbolic crucifixion, and ultimate defeat was portrayed symbolically when the bad people and their allies ritually killed Jesus on Good Friday. During the day of *"La Gloria"* or Holy Saturday, as dramatic events unfolded, flowers- representing good- were thrown at the evil ones. They ritually "killed" the evil *Fariseos* or Pharisees known as the *chapayekas*. Then, Jesus was resurrected as a baby. These were the main events of the drama, which ended on Easter Sunday coinciding with the Catholic ritual. There were ancient Yaqui symbols like flowers that are associated with the Blessed Virgin. During the days of ceremony and ritual, a *"manda"* or vow was made on behalf of a child or adult who was sick. A vow is usually fulfilled by service to the community. It was believed that if the person making the vow did not fulfill his ceremonial duties, he or she would be punished by sickness, accident or even death. This ritual has been carried out for centuries.

While it was fascinating to watch, it was clear that a translation of the Bible in the Yaqui language was needed. Our Christian friends in the Yaqui village had heard of John Dedrick of Wycliffe Bible Translators. There were rumors that he was doing a translation in Yaqui but nobody knew much about it. Since the Yaquis of Tucson had largely adopted Spanish as their language of preference, it seemed to be unnecessary. However, Bible translation had always been of interest to me, and from the beginning I realized just how important it was to extend God's word. It seemed right to start supporting Wycliffe Bible Translation financially so I joined what is called "Wycliffe Associates". This was a group of businessmen who gave of their time, talent and treasure to the cause of worldwide Bible translation.

Carla and I met Cameron Townsend near Tucson in 1981. The work of Bible Translation among minority groups held great interest for us. Uncle Cam, as he was lovingly called, dropped out of college and worked as a Bible salesman in Antigua, Guatemala. He eventually joined Central American Mission where he settled in a Kaqchikel community and continued to sell Spanish Bibles to the people. One day, a local Kaqchikel man who spoke a little Spanish said, "If your God is so smart, why hasn't he learned to speak my language?" That day changed everything. Since that Kaqchikel Indian first uttered that challenge, thousands of dedicated men and women have served the Lord with zeal to complete the task of Bible Translation. Over the next 14 years, Uncle Cam learned the Kaqchikel language and translated the written New Testament. The rest of the story is history. He went on to start a global organization that would change the world through Bible translation. That was the beginning of the modern missions movement. It reminded me of the Act 2:1-12 when the Holy Spirit came upon the believers at Pentecost and heard them speaking in all the languages of the unreached of that time. They heard the believers declaring the wonders of God in their own language. God was extending his message of hope in every language of the known world.

As the founder of Wycliffe Bible Translators, Uncle Cam often said: "Bible Translation is evangelization!" It took me some time to learn what he was talking about. Often young people came from the village as "informants". They learned about the contents of the Bible, and most were challenged by the Scripture even if not yet believers. Carla and I discovered that some of the first believers among unreached groups were the translator's "informants" or those who were native speakers. While their language was not yet put into written form, they were experts in the spoken language. As these "informants" became involved with the translation, they often came to know intimately the message of the Gospel. They were evangelized and discipled. So, Cameron Townsend words were true, "translation is evangelism." In fact, the idea was transformational to me and to Carla as well. As people got exposed to the written word, or the spoken words of Jesus, the process would change them. Even though it was men who wrote down the Scriptures, the Holy Spirit inspired them. The Bible itself says clearly that it is the inspired Word of God.

Bible Translation was a strategic key to reaching the unreached and the whole world. The Bible and God's life giving words needed to come alive in an important cultural context of a people group. Local speakers of a given language could be a "witness" to the others in a community. Once they receive this written translation, everyone is given the opportunity to either believe the Scriptures by faith or not. The fulfillment of Revelation 12:11 was now clear. *"They triumphed over him (the devil) by the blood of the Lamb (Jesus) and the word of their testimony;"* Further, we read from Scripture the very words of God, *"In the beginning was the Word, and the Word was with God, and the Word was God,"* wrote John about Jesus Christ. *"And the Word became flesh, and dwelt among us, and we saw His glory, glory as of the only begotten from the Father, full of grace and truth"* John 1:1, 14. These were and are the testimonies that I believed to be the true and faithful witnesses spoken by God himself.

With this involvement in Wycliffe Associates came another "Aha" moment. I saw clearly the link between Bible translation and becoming a witness for Christ. It came slowly, in incremental steps. But, the important thing became so clear to me. Scripture itself inspired by God himself was fundamental to reaching the unreached. I became connected to a group of people who shared this vision in Tucson. Carla and I became interested in a project of Wycliffe Mexico Branch to mobilize the body of Christ. Wycliffe Associates had purchased a very large tract of land to the north of Tucson. Wycliffe had been in Mexico as an organization since 1936 known as Summer

Institute of Linguistics (SIL). They had a contract with the government of Mexico to translate the Bible into every indigenous language in Mexico and provide reading primers and other literature. This arrangement had worked well since 1936 but it was now 1980 and things had changed substantially in Mexican politics and policy.

The Mexican Department of Indian Affairs, known as INI had reclaimed SIL's large center in Mexico City and all missionaries were asked to leave the country. As a result, many missionaries who had previously lived in Mexico were moving to Tucson. They had to get out immediately. Wycliffe/SIL Mexico Branch needed many volunteers to help build houses on their land near Tucson. Nearly one hundred translation teams were moving and Wycliffe Associates were bringing in large groups of volunteers from all over the country to construct missionary housing and an administrative center, a corporate worship center, along with a recording center where Bible portions and other audio materials could be recorded in different languages.

It was a massive project. Most of the volunteers were older retirees. They were free to do all the hard onsite construction work. Like many others, Carla and I gave to the project, prayed and kept track of the progress. Through it all, we were able to establish a new group of likeminded friends who were all committed to Bible translation. This move out of Mexico meant that translators, who had ongoing work there, had to finish their translations in a new U.S. location and setting. The solution was simple and came from God. The native language speakers or "informants", language associates, or co-translators would travel to Tucson and work for a few months at a time. The advantage was that they were free of distractions. They got travel and work visas from the U.S. Government. Wycliffe/ SIL was able to have a special relationship with immigration authorities. They often had someone to help language associates (native speakers) at the border to walk them though the process. Many Wycliffe/SIL translation teams were also able to travel to Mexico on a short-term basis and stay for short visits of a month or two. Between the two arrangements they overcame the huge challenge they had faced. God was at work to clear the way for Bible translation to continue on in every field of over one hundred translation projects. It was through this hard time that Carla and I got to know many translation teams and their co-translators. It was exciting to see all that God was doing in the hearts of these men and women, as well as what He was doing back home in the villages they came from.

In the fall of 1981 Carla and I were invited to a small community in Baja California by a pastor Pedro Carrillo. Through a series of circumstances, we traveled with close friends Jim Blakely and Doug Seaver to deliver food to a group of *Mixteco* believers in Colonia Distrito Federal. We had heard that the previous summer there was a devastating drought that had left many families without food and the basics for living. Carla and I, along with Jim and Doug purchased a truckload of food- mostly rice and beans- enough for nearly all the believers of this small community. Had we not arrived Pedro and his son would have taken their only cow to be slaughtered. It was their only source of milk but they were on the verge of starvation. There was great joy on Pedro's face when we pulled up. We started unloading the large sacks. They completely filled a room. It seemed as though God was miraculously multiplying an endless supply of food.

When we finished unloading, we celebrated with a dinner. Pedro's wife fixed us a wonderful Mexican dish consisting of the newly arrived rice and beans and we gave thanks to the Lord. When we were finishing up and preparing to leave, we all joined together in a time of prayer. During that time, we all held hands in a circle and Doug who has a special gift of healing from the Lord noticed that that Pedro's son had missing fingers on his left hand. Doug prayed and believed God could heal and restore his fingers. When we finished praying, Doug took his new gold watch off and gave it to the boy. As he slid the watch over his wrist, newly formed fingers appeared. God had restored his hand and we were all amazed. This was the first time I had witnessed such a miracle from God. Everyone was rejoicing in the Lord and there was unspeakable joy.

Every year, the Mixteco believers traveled nearly two thousand miles from their village in Oaxaca, Mexico to Pedro's border town near Mexicali, Mexico. They worked in the cotton fields by day and slept under the trees at night. Before the trip Carla and I were praying every day for God's sovereign will to be done in our lives. We trusted Him to lead us to be of service to others where ever we went. But, this trip was different. We could feel a strong presence of the Lord in a very special way during that trip.

We met Francisco and Antonia and their three children from the village of Manzanito. Francisco and his family went every year to work in Baja California to supplement his income. Back home in far away Oaxaca the corn that he grew was not enough to last the whole year. He earned enough working as a migrant worker in the fall and winter months to last the rest of the year. Annually he would struggle, torn between his familiar homeland, and the uncertain economic benefits of Baja California. They traveled in a group. While we were there, several Mixteco families came to pastor Pedro Carrillo's little Baptist church to worship God and sing their songs of praise in the Mixteco language. It was amazing and wonderful to hear believers sing to the Lord new songs of praise in their mother tongue. Never before had we been in contact with believers with such humility and sweet spirit. They were seeking a better home, better living conditions. They were strangers, travelers seeking a place to lay their heads.

After the church service, we all congregated outside in order to get to know our new friends from far away Oaxaca. I told them I very much liked their songs. Francisco and Antonia said, "Why don't you and your wife visit us in Oaxaca"? I was taken by surprise. I was not prepared for such an invitation. But Carla and I looked at each other with a smile on our faces and said, "Yes, that would be lovely". We went back home with a hand drawn map of the Oaxaca village of Manzanito and instructions on how to contact pastor Genaro of their little town. We told Francisco to expect us some time in June.

Carla and I wanted to have first hand experience of what it was like in the villages where they came from. We wanted to know what God was doing in their lives. We wanted to experience the joy of sharing life with the Mixtecos, to hear of their struggles and to share in their victories. We didn't know what to expect; we just wanted to go. God said, "Go into all the world". We would go and see what God was doing first hand.

13

Unknown Mexico

My Journal Entry June 11, 1982

Life changing events are sometimes very difficult to put into words. For me, Oaxaca meant going into an unknown world and Oaxaca changed my life. Leaving the familiarity of Tucson on a train I had never taken before, I sat wondering and anticipating what adventures God had in store for us. What kind of experiences would come our way? As I stood in the breezeway of the train's rear compartment, I watched pueblo after pueblo pass by. I didn't know the names of most, Carla would sometimes tell me the names she knew but everything I saw was new. For the first time I had an idea of how Abraham must have felt, led by God to a foreign place without clarity about the future.

Unknown Mexico seemed stark and bleak, dusty and at times unfriendly. But, inside of me was a new feeling of overwhelming joy. I can't describe it. I was on the adventure of a lifetime with God. Soon, we reached Mazatlán where I got off the train and bought a kilo of plátanos (bananas). It was beginning to get real hot! We met a young Mormon missionary who was being sent by his family to Cuernavaca to stay with a Mexican family to study Spanish for the summer.

As we left Mazatlan, I continued to enjoy our ride as the train swept along the shoreline with a full view of the beautiful, blue Pacific. I stood outside the cabin of the train, holding on to the rail guards, facing the wind, breathing the fresh air, and looking at the waves of the ocean crashing to shore. All too soon, the train took a turn and once again, we were traveling inland into stifling heat all the way to Tepic, Nayarit. I could feel the cool breezes of the mountainous area that surrounded Tepic. The train made a scheduled stop to pick up passengers. As I stepped out of the train compartment and into the breezeway there were two young Mexican men standing nearby. They were curious and wanted to know where I was from and why I was in Mexico. I was enjoying the visit and they helped me learn more Spanish words. They were very patient with me and willing to listen to the language errors I made so often. We laughed and I really was beginning to feel more comfortable with the Mexican people.

Back on the road again, the train took yet another turn, passing through several tunnels along the rough, mountainous terrain. I thought about how new and different it seemed, the sights, sounds and smells of a foreign land. We traveled on to Guadalajara at midnight. Only three hours late. Not bad for Mexican time. We quickly changed from the train to a bus, then on to Mexico City. On the bus we got some much needed sleep. Soon, we were in Mexico City, taking a speedy trip on the underground metro to our bus connection and on to Oaxaca. By this time, we had spent two full days on the train and bus to Mexico City.

At last, our destination seemed real even though we didn't know how far it was on to Oaxaca. Oh Lord, the bus was filled to capacity. Luckily, we got on early and were able to sit up front, next to the driver, another small miracle from God. We told the driver that we wanted to get off in Oaxaca City, uncertain when we would arrive there. The bus driver was very friendly and he played "marimba" music over the loud speakers the entire way. We made the long, arduous, and frightening trip through the mountains. The driver drove very fast around the curves. When he would reach the summit of a long climb up a mountain pass, he would "cross" himself, and say a quick prayer. The gearbox of the transmission would grind and groan, then shift to low gear. Down the long road we went, our knees knocking all the way. Oh my God! I'm so glad you go with us!

Finally arriving at nightfall, we were dirty and tired, but we were thankful. We had reached our destination. I saw many unique indigenous people who were wearing native, colorful costumes. They were huddled together waiting at the bus station bound for unknown places. Most were very poor, surviving the harsh economic circumstances of Mexico, living a way of life so foreign to me. They would stare at us and I was embarrassed to be an American. I felt their angry eyes on me expressing envy, bitterness and resentment. I felt helpless and confused, not knowing what to do about the poverty that each one faced. It was hopeless, what could I do about their condition? I was simply a symbol of all their economic hardships.

We checked into a very old hotel, which dated from the year 1580 when it was a Catholic Convent. The hotel was restful, welcoming and picturesque. Its architecture was from 16th Century Spain. It was so charming with its lush tropical gardens, surrounded by mountains with cloud filled, pine covered peaks. Carla and I were relieved to catch up on our sleep. We were both thankful that we had completed the long journey. We dined that evening in a garden under the stars while the smooth and melodic "Trio Marino" played a Spanish love song. The night of rest ended so quickly.

14

Call of the Conch

The following day we were off to continue our quest. Where could we find the Mixtecos of Manzanito? How could we get there? We found a small shop where a brother named Artémio was of assistance. He told us that pastor Genaro who we were looking for had died four months before. Oh Lord, my heart fell to the floor. This pastor was a key connection to the Mixtecos. However, Artémio told us that another pastor had read our letter and knew of our desire to get Bibles in the Mixteco language to our dear brothers in a remote region of the Sierra Madre Mountains.

This pastor was José Santiago Martinez. The next day, José made arrangements for a bus ride out to the village of Mitla to visit with the translator at the Summer Institute of Linguistics. John Daly and his wife Margaret were the translators of a dialect of Mixteco near to Manzanito. We learned that the New Testaments in Mixteco were packed away in storage in Mitla. I thought it strange that "The Word of God" would be locked away and hidden from the Mixtecos. But, in fairness to John, he was completely unaware that this group existed. We arrived midmorning and talked a while with Searle Hoogshagen a translator for yet another language group called the Mixes. He was very kind and helpful and together we found the New Testaments in Mixteco, packed several boxes of the hardback books on to the bus and we were off again to Oaxaca City to make arrangements and to buy bus tickets to Manzanito.

By now we were staying in the humble home of Pastor José, his wife Balbina and his in-laws on the outskirts of Oaxaca City. The following morning José got us up early. We boarded a *"segunda"*, a rattletrap bus to the mountain village of Contreras. We arrived there three hours later. Brother Tomás of Manzanito met up with us in Contreras and carried a portion of the New Testaments in a fiber bag strapped to his forehead. We strapped the eight boxes left on to two donkeys. We ascended the high mountain range along with a group of other families who had been buying supplies and were now returning home. It was a four-hour hike to the village. Each Mixteco family seemed so unified. Father, mother, children all together, each one bearing his own burden, even the little ones. Everyone was friendly even though they all knew we were "gringos". I felt more at ease. God made a path to the people of Manzanito.

Before we arrived, we heard the trumpeting echo of the conch shell announcing our arrival to all the surrounding hamlets. It was an ancient sound. The mountain villages had used the conch shell since pre-Columbian times. The sound echoed throughout the high mountains and valley. It was a signal for all the men and women to gather together. The sound of the conch shell was also a signal to Carla and me as well. I was feeling the full time call to missions deep inside me. This calling would need time for definition and clarity, but I heard it for the first time in the mountains of Oaxaca. I heard the voices of many unreached peoples around the world crying out. Our calling would be tested in the fires of doubt and fears, but I heard His voice, calling out to me. Once again, he was talking to me as God spoke to Moses, or David, or to all who hear his voice. Jesus said, *"My sheep listen to my voice; I know them, and they follow me." John 10:27*

As we got closer to the village we could see the beautiful faces of every member of the Mixteco tribe of that village, men, wives and children. All of them seemed overjoyed to see us. After greeting us the men of the town gathered together to discuss plans to bring a road to Manzanito from the nearest town of Contreras, which is fifteen miles away. Currently, it was a four-hour walk nearly straight uphill. The road would have to be cleared by hand.

While the men discussed their problems concerning the road, Carla and I began reciting the letters of the Mixteco alphabet, following along in a simple alphabet book with letters and short sentences. The younger school aged children huddled up nearby to catch a glimpse of the magic book with written words which were spoken every day, but never before seen in written form. Carla and I will never forget their faces as I turned the pages. They seemed truly excited and eager to learn. While I didn't speak Mixteco, we had a pre-recorded tape from the translator clearly pronouncing all the words and phrases in their language. I had recorded it with John Daly before I left for Oaxaca. It was another example of God's provision.

After the lesson the children ran off to play a game of marbles, but one young man stayed behind to talk. He asked me about the U.S. and what it was like. Esteban was a young man of about fifteen. We met him for the first time near Mexicali when he migrated the previous fall with the others of the tribe to work in the cotton fields. It seemed clear from his questions that God was dealing with him about his future. I asked him if he still had the Spanish/English Bible I had given him the previous year. He said yes, that he was still learning English but he had no one to practice with.

Many of the believers had given up hope that we would really come to visit them, until Antonia's dream the night before. In her dream, she saw us coming over the mountain to give them a gift. Little did she know that very day they would receive the greatest gift of all, the Word of God. I asked Esteban if he thought he could learn to read and write Mixteco. He was sure he could. I encouraged him to spend his time learning to read Mixteco. "These are your people and your people need the written word. Someday this effort will become more fruitful than learning to speak English." He agreed, and later that evening Esteban was first in line to buy the Mixteco New Testament we had brought to the village. That night, the pitch pine torches glowed up and down the mountainside as Mixtecos from far and wide came to greet us. Much to our surprise, many people lined up to obtain a Mixteco New Testament for a few pesos each. The thick, hardback books we carried over the mountain range represented twenty years of sacrificial work of the SIL translators.

The brothers and sisters cried with passionate emotion at the acquisition of such a precious treasure book. But I later learned that only a few people could read this important book written in their own language. There was a three-hour dedication service in a dimly lit adobe building set precariously off the side of the mountain. One by one, every Mixteco New Testament was distributed. Some would have to wait for another time. There were sad looks for those who were too late. The service ended at midnight. The New Testaments we brought seemed like such a small token of our love and affection. To the Mixteco believers it seemed we had brought life. Carla and I were overwhelmed with the gratitude they expressed. We were standing at the door when one elderly Mixteca woman gave me a kiss on my cheek. Despite their extremely reserved manner, she wanted to express her profound thanks. It was the end of a very long day but a very rewarding day. I wrote in my journal that night "How rare are such purpose filled days."

The next day, a group of believers were looking at the newly arrived New Testaments. One young man who was holding the book upside down drew closer to me. He said as he pointed at the book, "What language is this written in, I don't recognize it?" I was taken by surprise. Maybe he had not attended the dedication last night where everything about the book was carefully explained by pastor José. I patiently explained to him that the book was written in Mixteco. I went on to say that a man spent twenty years translating this book in "your language" and it was written for the whole community to read and to enjoy it. He then said, "I can't read, sir!" This was a problem we had not expected. We didn't realize that in their poverty and lack of education most people could not read. This needed prayer and direction from God. But, Carla and I took this challenge seriously. It was to become central to all that lie ahead.

Eating Mixteco food was not as difficult as I had feared. Sister Vivian attended to almost everything. She spoke Spanish well, unusual for Mixteca women who were monolingual in their mother tongue. Rising before sunrise to kill a chicken, Vivian started early cooking rice, black beans and tortillas. She served us in ways I was not accustomed to. She was completely attentive to our every need. Most of the time food was prepared and eaten on the floor without a table. Carla, José and I were treated differently. We were honored guests and given a table to eat on and sometimes they took food to our room. In every way, our Mixteco brothers gave us all they had. I was humbled and taken back by their kindness; it was hard to be treated so special.

At our first breakfast we talked about the many problems facing Manzanito. There was the lack of a generator for electricity, the need of a road, and issues with poor crops. Many issues were on the minds of everyone at breakfast. We talked of their plan to complete the small schoolhouse now under construction. There were two full time teachers spending the entire school year in one, small room, a dirt floor shed. They were trying to teach and help the children learn. Something had to be done. The young men of the village however had a good and achievable plan. I had to leave all their problems and worries in God's able hands. "God, give me the grace to trust you. You alone will take on the tremendous burdens they carry". I wanted to help, but God was saying that He would take care of Manzanito.

On our last day in the village two of the men volunteered to go down the mountain to Contreras with us helping to carry our backpacks. As we started our descent down the steep canyon wall, I paused a while to get just one more glimpse of Manzanito. It was probably the quiet, the calm setting of the moment that helped me draw closer to the Lord. I reflected on our visit. We had completed our goal and my inner man leaped for joy. How wonderful is our God. How great is our God. I gave thanks for the life changing opportunity we had in this village.

From that day forward, the call of the conch shell would symbolize a significant turning point in my life. The sound of the conch shell reminded me of the wonderful people we had just met but most of all it reminded me of his call to serve. I realized more than ever, that this would never have happened had Jesus not given His life for each of us. Jesus was the number one priority in my life. My heartfelt friendship and common bond of unity with the Mixtecos was in Christ. These experiences would guide me for all of my days. I realized whether one is rich or poor, from Manzanito, the U.S.A. or any place on earth; we are all one in Christ because our citizenship is in heaven.

15

Return to Manzanito

My Missionary Journal Entry- June 12, 1983

With great uncertainty and concern, the decision to leave for Mexico while my father was very ill was a difficult one. The Scripture that God gave me was very significant in making the decision to leave. It was confirmed the evening we arrived in Oaxaca. I John 20:21 "Peace I give to you, even as the father sent me, so I send you." I knew my real father was sending me out. We were following up last years visit. When we arrived in Oaxaca City we found our way to the small church in La Colonia Montezuma where we met our friend and mentor José Santiago preaching and teaching a group of Mixtecos from Manzanito along with some other people in the neighborhood. As José closed the service he asked Carla and I to sing a song that touched us deeply; so we sang a song from Romans 14:8: "If we live, we live for the Lord; and if we die, we die for the Lord. So, whether we live or die, we belong to the Lord." This was all in Spanish. All of a sudden that particular Scripture put everything in such clear perspective. My father's grave illness was heavy on my heart but God was saying to me, "Give your father's illness to me." After the service our reunion with José was a very joyous one. We had surprised him walking into the middle of Sunday night services. Our letters had not arrived and he was not expecting us until the following month.

Foremost in our minds and hearts was the problem of literacy we had learned about the year before. We had a strategy in mind but we had to work out the details. The next day, we left Oaxaca City for Mitla. There we were to meet Roger Reek and his wife Marylyn. We went there in search of a place to record the Mixteco language. He directed us to Glenn Stairs and his wife Emily who showed us a house. I felt the Lord directing us to this house across the street from the S.I.L. (Summer Institute of Linguistics) a compound on the outskirts of Mitla, a small town east of Oaxaca City. There we were kindly received and very graciously offered this small house to use for a week or ten days until we could complete recording Ephesians with brother Marcelino. He was a native speaker of Mixteco and one of several people we met the year before. We worked most of the day preparing the room and sound proofing the area we were recording in. We finished for the day and we took a much-needed rest sitting out in the patio. I felt the cool breeze dance across the lush tropical garden. As the trees rustled overhead, we heard the distant sound of thunder and lightning strikes. The evening ended with much needed rain.

We awoke after a good night's rest to cloudy skies, cool weather, and fresh air. We took a taxi to Teotitlan del Valle and found a uniquely designed rug for our house. It would also be useful for sound proofing the recording room. I was so thankful for all those back home who were praying because the pieces of the puzzle were fitting together ever so perfectly. I called home to the U.S. No news about my dad and that was good news. We began recording with a prayer. We all prayed together that the Lord would bless our time together and the words Marcelino spoke on tape would be clear to the listeners. It was a special day when we began to record the book of Ephesians in Mixteco.

We worked several days on the recording without much difficulty with the equipment but Marcelino's reading skills were poor. The Mixteco language is tonal. Because of the tonal markings, written Mixteco looks very different from written Spanish. In fact, it was so difficult it looked like a musical score written on the page. Considering everything, he did very well but every sentence was a struggle. He had to take some time trying to figure out what the translation of Ephesians was saying, then practice saying it several times until it sounded smooth. Then we would record, but sometimes Lino (his nickname) would have to record it again. So, between learning what the verse said, practice time, and recording time it took a whole day to record a single chapter of Ephesians.

Another challenge was that the apostle Paul wrote the letter of Ephesians in complicated, very long sentences. We needed lots of prayer to get through it. On top of every thing else, I got very sick the last few days of recording. I had fever and diarrhea and didn't sleep hardly at all, so when morning would arrive I was already exhausted. Needless to say, my performance was not good and I was short tempered and impatient with Lino. He went on in spite of my impatience. One afternoon my brother called me from Las Vegas. It was Friday June 17th. We had lost my father due to complications that had set in after his recent heart surgery. Bob said the life support systems that had been on dad for the past week or so were removed; the doctors could not justify continued use any longer. He only lasted five seconds after the machines were removed. I will miss my dad very much. God gave me a Scripture that I needed: "My grace is sufficient for you, for my power is made perfect in weakness". 2 Corinthians 12:9. Once again He spoke to me and I released my dad to God. "He is in your hands O' God". My dad never found redemption to my knowledge, and thank God, I'm not his judge. I felt so bad that I was not there when my father died, but I trusted God to give me grace. I had grown accustomed to missing my dad for most of my life. "I love you dad, I wish we could have spent more time together." He was now in Jesus' hands. By now, I had long forgiven my dad for all that had happened between us. We had reconciled and made our peace years before. It was the end of a sad chapter.

I thought back to dad's actions of the past, the day he left us at grandma's house. It occurred to me that perhaps he realized that his presence in our lives was not in the best interest of us boys. Perhaps he wanted us to have more than he could give us. Maybe he was a bigger person, a more selfless person than I gave him credit for. Love sometimes provokes the strangest actions.

The next day, we got off to a very early start after a good night's rest. The illness I had seemed to pass. We finished up the sixth and final chapter of Ephesians. It went so well that we were finished by mid-afternoon. After we completed our task, we were so happy that we got down on our knees and thanked the Lord and had a good time of prayer. We took the master copy of Ephesians into Oaxaca City and made twenty copies to take back to Manzanito. We set our alarm for 4:30 am (ouch) to catch the Contreras bus. José was there promptly to meet us at the station. Our arrival in the village was again announced by the sounding of the conch shell and many from the village were standing near the church to greet us. It was very difficult to hold back tears of joy. It was wonderful to see them once again, to see their happy faces. Tomás was there, Lino, Miguel and Vivian, Francisco and his wife Antonia, Esteban, Pedro and so many others, some familiar, some not. After greeting everyone we all sat down to eat and enjoy the company of old friends. We walked up to Lino's home and greeted his wife and children, and we saw his humble house. Lino was so glad to see us because he had been waiting for us to arrive. I was so touched by his love and affection.

The next day, José called an early 8:00 A.M. meeting of the leaders of the church and any others who wanted to participate in the literacy class Carla was to give that day. To our surprise, leaders from four different places were there. Nico and Lino from Manzanito and Contreras, Isadoro Pérez from San Mateo Tepantepec, José and many more representing the migrant believers who were now living in Colonia Montezuma, in Oaxaca City and now attending the church in the city. It was amazing that so many from different dialects of Mixteco were present.

We learned of the different dialects when we were recording with Lino. Each town spoke differently but they could understand each other when speaking. Their dialect was their identity. It was very confusing to us outsiders. However, in spite of the differences, the literacy lesson on transition from Spanish reading to Mixteco went extremely well and all were very eager to learn. Nico-a new pastor assigned to Manzanito-was very unsure of himself in the beginning, but by the time we finished the day he was the best student. The recording we had made was an aide to learning to read. Students followed along in their written New Testament while listening to Ephesians. Reading the passage was followed by discussions about what they learned. The big question was, "Could they sustain the training received without Carla there to lead them to the next step?"

The lessons were over in about four hours. We realized that God was touching the village in a new and special way. Our dream of Bible literacy had begun. It was decided that Lino would give the lesson the next day while Carla could be on hand to answer any questions. We hoped this was the beginning of a sustainable literacy program that would continue long after we had left and Lino seemed to be the person to continue the lessons. Nico was the new pastor of Manzanito. José anointed Nico with oil and installed him as pastor in place of the late pastor Genaro. It was a new era for Manzanito. A new pastor was appointed and a new program of Biblical literacy was becoming a reality.

Days later, as we began our long walk out of the village, we pondered the many triumphs of our journey, but also the failures and difficulties. Everyone exalted the Lord that day. We would carry the events of Manzanito deep within our hearts all of our life. However, Carla and I went back to Arizona with many questions on our mind. While our hearts were telling us to go back to Manzanito and continue the literacy program, practical reality told us that the Mexican government would not give us residency to stay there because of the new policy toward Wycliffe/SIL and foreigners, and especially "gringos" from the U.S.A. Once again we placed our future in the hands of the Lord. We trusted him in all things. God would have a plan for us.

The intense days of recording Ephesians in the Mixtec language had hardly left time to think about the death of my father. When I returned home, my dad was on my mind and my heart. He was only sixty-two when he left this world. I wanted to say so many things to him. His sudden departure was a reminder of just how short this life can be. We don't know how many days we have on this place called earth. My dad did not live out his days trusting in Jesus. He was not much of an example to me or anyone else. I knew that, but in all honesty I couldn't help thinking, "Where is dad now"? Thank God, I could trust God with that too. This was a watershed moment for me. I had to ask myself some very difficult questions. Had I completely forgiven my father for abandoning mother, my brothers and me? The many times dad and I met to recall the Krupp Diamond heist flashed through my mind. I thought of all the pain and suffering my brothers and I experienced. A verse came to me from Matthew 18:21 which says, "Then Peter came up and said to him, "Lord, how often will my brother sin against me, and I forgive him? Up to seven times? Jesus answered, "I tell you, not seven times, but seventy-seven times." I didn't know how many times my father had sinned against me, but it no longer mattered. Love covers a multitude of sins. Suddenly, I no longer felt abandoned and forsaken. I found my heavenly father, I had totally forgiven my earthly father and I had peace and joy from within.

16

A Seed Was Planted, a Time of Transition

When we returned from Oaxaca, we told all our friends about the many amazing experiences we had and the successful recording of Ephesians and the literacy classes in Mixteco that were now well on their way to helping the church of Manzanito. We held great hopes for what was started and prayed regularly for them. At the same time, I had to tell our friends about my father's death while I was recording in Mexico. The death of my father was another point of decision. "If I have only one life to live", I prayed, "let it be a life dedicated to you and your Kingdom". It was just a tiny mustard seed at this point, the seed that was first planted in Oaxaca. The Holy Spirit reminded me of the Scripture in John 20:21: "Peace be with you! As the Father has sent me, I am sending you". Here was another miracle in my life, a life-changing miracle.

I had no formal theological training. I hadn't been to Bible School or to seminary. This concerned me and was on my mind after we got back from Oaxaca. Should I go or should I not? Is the Holy Spirit a sufficient source for training or did I need more training to adequately serve the Lord? The question would linger for the next three years as I pondered the different options. I thought about the Scripture verse of *Acts 4:13* "*When they saw the courage of Peter and John and they realized that they were ordinary men, they were astonished and took note that these men had been with Jesus.*" Three years passed before I would finally decide. Meanwhile, there was plenty to do. There was my work at the Star and Citizen Newspaper, studying Spanish at the University of Arizona, and ongoing projects at Wycliffe Catalina Branch Tucson. I read many books on the lives of Wycliffe missionaries and other great missionaries of the past who were worthy to emulate. There was plenty of time to find my way. Carla and I were weighing the cost, praying for guidance, and talking to Wycliffe missionaries with whom we were working in Mexico.

Meanwhile, Carla and I also had started a Bible Study in our home that was a big encouragement to us. In fact, it provided weekly spiritual guidance and support. We had met these friends and partners in the Gospel in the early 1980's when we were first married. They prayed for us when we went to Baja California and to Oaxaca for the first time. We shared with them our victories and defeats particularly during our trips to Oaxaca. In all, there were seven-eight people who formed the core of the group. Gary and Nancy Lovelace were also a big support and help. Everyone prayed wholeheartedly and engaged with everything we were doing in missions. We were all very close and we celebrated holidays and special occasions with them on a regular basis. They were prayer partners from the beginning and without prayer nothing can happen. Also, our church Abundant Life Christian Fellowship provided the guidance that we were seeking from a larger corporate body. The Pastor, Dan Gill gave us much needed spiritual inspiration and additional counsel. We weighed the cost of being a disciple of Jesus Christ and giving our lives for the cause of Christ.

Then in 1984 we met Erik and Teri Powell, missionaries with Navajo Gospel Mission. They had been working in Northern Mexico and among other things were engaging in a survey of all the unreached groups of that region. Erik and Teri lived in Bisbee, Arizona, going in and out of Mexico from there. It was shocking to learn from Erik that so many groups of indigenous people of Mexico were considered "unreached" and many were unengaged, indigenous groups without a missionary presence. Erik and I had many more discussions about unreached people and the challenges these people groups were facing.

We learned a great deal from Ralph Winter (1925-2009) founder of the US Center for World Mission (USWM). He was a proponent of the cause of unreached people. He became widely known after presenting his paper at Billy Graham's Lausanne Congress on World Evangelization in July 1974 when 2,430 participants with 570 observers from 150 countries descended on Lausanne, Switzerland. Ralph's paper it is said by many mission leaders kicked off a new era in the frontier mission movement. I subscribed to his monthly magazine "Frontier Missions" and stayed connected with occasional visits to their campus in Pasadena, California to learn all I could. Through the USWM I began to learn exactly what specific problems and challenges pioneer missionaries faced.

Our experience in Mexico resonated with many of the things that he was saying in what was later documented in books about Ralph Winter. The first and most obvious was that missionaries needed to be aware of the enormous cultural distances and that missionaries needed to find new ways to effectively present the Gospel so that it could be communicated easily across the cultural divide. This was significant to me. He was saying that most missionaries were preaching the Gospel in areas that had long been reached, that more attention was needed on the unreached and unengaged. Another fact that impressed me was his advocacy for a non-western missions force that was beginning to take hold. Further, we had already faced the problem of syncretism and distortion of the Gospel among the Yaquis and Mixtecos but Ralph Winter put a bright spotlight on this too. He was clear that missionaries needed to carefully examine their methods and practices as they planted the church among the unreached. But most of all he encouraged the formation of new mission agencies with new methods that would take into consideration all the needs of the unreached, and that stuck with me most.

Considering the proximity of Mexico to the U.S. it was surprising that there were still over fifty groups with the official status of "unreached or unengaged". On the other hand, when one considers the hostile attitude of the Mexican government toward any foreign presence in the country it was easy to understand. We prayed for guidance for God to send the right people.

17

Unreached Peoples

One such group of "unreached" was the Tarahumara or *Raramuri* (those who run fast). They lived in the mountains of Chihuahua, Mexico. Erik told us that he became aware of this group during his survey of the area. We told Erik of our experiences among the Mixtecos of Oaxaca and our desire to see them become literate, to have access to the Word of God. We told him of the enormous challenges that we faced attempting to share the Gospel when the majority of people were of oral tradition, had no formal literacy and lived in a remote part of Mexico. We had quite a discussion about the need for literacy for all unreached peoples. What was that the best way to reach these people? Was it necessary for a person to become literate in order to become a follower of Jesus Christ? Then the discussion turned to the newly released "Jesus Film".

I told Erik of my background in film production and my willingness to contact Campus Crusade and explore the possibilities of making the film in the Tarahumara language. This was the very film Carla and I had seen on our first date. It was taken entirely form the Gospel of Luke. Wycliffe Bible Translators had sent Kenneth Hilton to the Tarahumara people in about 1939 when the U.S. and Mexico had a better relationship. He lived and worked among them for many years and had completed a translation of the New Testament in the 1960's. So, Erik and I were confident that we could get help and perhaps we could have the "Jesus Film" available for evangelism and discipleship. Our experience had already shown literacy was a task that needed time, and time wasn't something we felt we had a lot of. We didn't have enough experience with literacy to know exactly what to do, but the Jesus Film seemed to be an exciting opportunity, worth the time and energy to experiment with. We knew they were oral people with oral traditions. Maybe the film would become the breakthrough we were all praying for.

The following week, I called the Jesus Film headquarters and the secretary answered the phone. I briefly explained who I was, and expressed my desire to speak to the person in charge of translation of the film. She yelled loudly across the room "Hey, Paul there's a guy on the phone that wants to talk to you." It was Paul Eshleman, Vice President of Campus Crusade for Christ and founder of "The Jesus Film Project." I explained to him that we needed the film in the Tarahumara language and asked when could we get a copy. He clarified that the film was only available in major languages like English, Spanish, French and a few others and the minority languages were not due to be translated for many years.

I had a flash of inspiration from the Holy Spirit. I explained to Paul that I had film experience as a broadcast producer.

"Could I get the English script and start the translation or dubbing from Kenneth Hilton's New Testament of Luke in the Tarahumara language?" Paul agreed on the spot, and we received the English to Spanish script in the mail the following week. We managed to get a copy of the New Testament and made Xerox copies of Luke in Tarahumara cutting and pasting in passages along side of the Spanish translation. Each scene was carefully timed to fit the visual and audio into the time needed.

Our home Bible study group got involved too. Many, many hours were spent on each page, pasting and checking every scene in the story of Jesus from Luke. Final copies were made and again checked for accuracy. We ordered four reels of 16 mm film in Spanish, parts one to four. I bought used Nagra professional reel-to-reel recording equipment. We also bought a projector to use in the village in order to compare the Tarahumara narration against the Spanish. We made arrangements with Erik and Teri and left for a great adventure in the Sierra Tarahumara during August monsoon season. We were excited that for the first time we would experience this unreached group that we had heard so much about. We let most of our friends and prayer partners know of our plans. Everyone would be praying and asking God for favor.

Erik and Teri brought a generator and a four-wheel drive vehicle filled with camping gear for several weeks. I took off a month of vacation time and Carla was on summer break from teaching. We traveled together from Bisbee, Arizona and crossed the border at Naco, Sonora. We drove two days, one day on paved roads, and then another full day high in the mountains on dirt roads used by logging trucks. It was a long, hard and dusty road to Samachique, Chihuahua the heartland of the Tarahumaras.

Because there was no communication to the village like telephones, text, or email, we went all that way by faith. None of us had any idea what we would find or if anyone could help us translate the Jesus Film. When we got there, we learned that the Wycliffe Translator, Kenneth Hilton had left the area many years ago and his co-translator named Rámon Lopez was out of town. My heart sank to the floor, but it was suggested by someone that Ramon's son Eduardo might help us. He worked at the local sawmill and as foreman he had flexible hours and indeed, he agreed to record for us. Wow! God's provision turned out to be a complete blessing as Eduardo was a brilliant reader and a dedicated, hard worker.

He gave us an empty log cabin where we could record and sleep. That first night, Eduardo asked us to show the film to him and his family in Spanish in order to become familiar with the contents. He and his family had never seen it before. Many of the leaders of the Tarahumara people were bi-lingual. The Spanish language was a necessity especially for leaders and their families. Eduardo was the perfect person to do this project at a moment's notice. We could communicate with him in Spanish, and he and several Tarahumara men took turns checking the recordings for accuracy. God was at work again.

It took five long days and evenings to record the two-hour movie narration. Timing was always very tricky. There were interruptions to gas up the generator that provided power, as there was no electricity in the region. Electricity, gasoline, sewer, and running water were unavailable, even unknown to the Tarahumara. The long verses of Luke in the Tarahumara language did not fit with the fast moving visuals, nevertheless most of the time the words and the picture came together to the second and if the scene didn't fit Eduardo would re-work the text to fit exactly. We wrapped up the recording of our first minority language film. We gave thanks to the Lord and headed back to Arizona to post-produce the film.

Back home, there remained lots of work to do. The Jesus Film office sent us the music and effects track that arrived from England. At home, I cut the narration track into the music and effects track so that it would sound natural. The sound effects needed to be low when Eduardo was speaking, and the music would go up in between. The narration track needed to sound smooth and match the music track. When this process was completed, I finished the final cut of the film at the University of Arizona film department, a handy connection from my days at Aztec Films. I worked on this during evenings because of my job at the newspaper. It took until the end of January 1985 to complete it.

We planned a return to the Tarahumara tribal area for Holy Week of that year. We chose Easter because the tribe as-cribed special significance to Easter largely because of the Jesuit teachings of the 17th and 18th Centuries. It was similar to what had occurred among the Yaquis of Sonora and Tucson. The Tarahumara lived in isolation, in Mexico's Grand Canyon called the *Barranca del Cobre* or Copper Canyon. They were a sturdy and independent people, but very shy with outsiders. There were about fifty thousand Tarahumaras in the highlands and more lived in the lowland areas. The highland country was a very beautiful, rugged, pine wilderness; a place of cave dwellings, waterfalls, and flower covered hilly meadows and colorfully dressed Tarahumara people. They were true artisans: weavers of belts, makers of baskets and pottery, and carvers of wooden violins. The land they lived in was cold, dry and harsh especially in the wintertime. Easter was a time of transitional weather. That year, Easter time in Samachique was especially harsh. A cold wind was blowing across the valley. Evening was the only time to hold an event like this but it meant open-air meetings in the bitter cold outdoors. Despite the weather, over one hundred people who lived scattered thought the hills showed up for the premier showing of the Jesus Film. We had given some thought to how we would show the film in an outdoor setting. Fires were lit in several locations to keep the crowd warm on this brisk spring night. We also came prepared with a large portable screen, outdoor speakers, amplifier, and projector. Also, we set up tables with the New Testaments and Scripture portions for sale at prices the Tarahumaras could afford. If they had been given free, they would not have been valued and possibly tossed aside. As it was we were unaware how few could read.

Ramón and his son Eduardo were on hand but had been skeptical. They had pastored the tiny local church for many years and had seen North Americans come and go. Most of their promises of help and materials had not been kept. But this time it was different. They saw that we had done what we said we would do. The people were visibly shaken by the cruelty and pain they witnessed as Jesus was put to death on the cross. The Tarahumara feared death intensely, sending their dead to the afterlife with days of elaborate ceremonies. When the film ended, Ramon asked those interested in knowing more about Jesus to come to the lights stretched across the front of the film sight. No one came. But, twenty-five or thirty Tarahumaras lingered and sat talking quietly while they warmed themselves. It was as if they were waiting for something. They stood by while Ramón stayed by the fire talking with only a few teenage boys asking some questions.

Why had the people not come to the lights when Ramón asked? It was later made clear that the invitation made them feel singled out. In their culture the only time a person is singled out from the group is for punishment or tribal ostracism. One young man spoke to me the next day. He wanted to know where the people came from who had killed Jesus. I answered him and then I asked him if he understood the sacrifice Jesus made for us. "I must offer goats, burros and chickens to *"Onoruame"* (our father the sun) so that my crops will not fail and God will not be angry with me," he said. "That's what Jesus has done for us", I said. "He was the last sacrifice needed for all men, for all time." *(Excerpts from "I Just Saw Jesus" by Paul Eschelman.)*

There were communication obstacles to overcome in the film. For example, there is no word for "cross"; we had to borrow a word from Spanish. There is also no word for "angel". Many more such borrowed words were used like blood sacrifice, redemption and the list goes on and on. The Jesuit priests had introduced the concept of the cross in the eighteenth century though it was not totally understood. The culture had accepted making the sign of the cross. They wore rosaries with small crucifixes and used crosses ceremonially for sickness. Small crosses were wrapped with the dead and placed at the grave. These became bridges that we would use to communicate the full message of the gospel.

The four cardinal directions were an important part of daily life and ceremony among the Tarahumara. all food and drink were dedicated to the four directions. The dedication consisted of raising the bowls of food three times in each direction, east, west, north and south. They drank *tesguino*-a corn liquor-at all ceremonies and community events. The tesquino drinking occasions were frequent, and the drunkenness of both men and women was an enormous problem for the community. It was so pervasive it had become a real problem for Rámon and the local church as well.

The sacrifice of animals was a big part of the native *fiesta,* especially at Easter. It was similar to that of the Yaquis but different. A goat or cow was never killed without dancing the *"dutuburi";* the sacrifice could be whatever a family could afford to offer to *"onoruame"* or great father, or literally "our father the sun." They made sacrifices of the meat of goats, cows, chickens, rabbits and squirrels, but not dogs or pigs. The ceremony offered the blood of an animal. It was concluded with dancing the *"yumari".* These too were *"bridges"* of communication that we would use in the future. We used their concepts of sacrifice to help the Tarahumara people to understand the God of the Bible. We learned many things about Tarahumara worldview, especially their understanding of spiritual things. I learned for the first time that anthropologists considered them "animists". They believed gods and spirits lived in the wind, rocks, the trees, in fact in nearly everything.

We packed up the next day after the film showing. We had heard there was a Mexican missionary named Alfredo Guerrero that was in the village of *Choguita,* a traditional town accessible by dirt road hours from where we were in

Samachique. He had been working in this area for 5 years. He heard about the film and had sent word for us to come, as he was anxious to show the film. Alfredo and his family had been living among the Tarahumaras and sharing the gospel in this small community of about one hundred families spread out over a large geographic area. Alfredo had been preaching to a small group that had been attending meetings but still needed to know more about Jesus and he felt that the Jesus Film in their language would help them gain the complete understanding that they needed to make a commitment.

We showed the film in four small *"rancherias"* over a couple of days. Large groups of over one hundred attended. A core group of ten committed believers came from those initial showings. The Jesus Film completely changed Alfredo's ministry. He saw the value of oral communication of the Scriptures in the mother tongue language and built on teaching the Jesuits brought many centuries before. We had all worked successfully as a team to bring the message of Jesus to a remote and harsh land filled with poverty and tradition, but we found out that in some ways their needs were the same as ours; they needed to find meaning and hope for their lives brought to them through Jesus' message: *"Come to me, all you who labor and are heavy laden, and I will give you rest." Matthew 11:28* Before we left the area, Alfredo and his family and the film team gathered to give thanks to the Lord. Over time, God used the film to make a huge impression on the Tarahumara people; many more new believers discovered faith and many lives were transformed. However, there were still questions. Carla and I sat together to assess all that God had done. Although many came to faith as a result of the Jesus Film, we

were troubled about how these new believers would reproduce that model involving technology-projectors, trucks, gas
and so forth- independent of the missionaries? These questions would linger for several years.

18

A Big Vision

Once again, we came back from the Sierra Tarahumara in the spring of 1985 content but with a lot of questions lingering. It was apparent by the people's enthusiastic response that while progress was good, we all agreed that a lot more time needed to be invested for a church to be established among the Tarahumara people. Ramón and his son Eduardo had labored many years; they were one with the tribe and they had a deep commitment to the language, the people and to the gospel and yet their results were insignificant. When we got back home we prayed and asked God to show us the way to reach those tender hearts. We needed a clear vision for the future. I came to love and appreciate this old hymn of the church that says it all.

> Be Thou my Vision, O Lord of my heart
> Naught be all else to me, save that Thou art
> Thou my best Thought, by day or by night
> Waking or sleeping, Thy presence my light

Be Thou my Wisdom, and Thou my true Word
I ever with Thee and Thou with me, Lord
Thou my great Father, I Thy true son
Thou in me dwelling, and I with Thee one
Riches I heed not, nor man's empty praise
Thou mine Inheritance, now and always
Thou and Thou only, first in my heart
High King of Heaven, my Treasure Thou art
High King of Heaven, my victory won
May I reach Heaven's joys, O bright Heav'n's Sun
Heart of my own heart, whate'er befall
Still be my Vision, O Ruler of all

Carla and I were bound together by love of God and love for one another. Together, we would set a course for the rest of our lives. There was no turning back. God was our vision; He himself was the beat of our heart. This song says it all. God, be my vision, present in every thought. Be my light, my wisdom and my great Father. Thank you for dwelling in me. You are my riches, wealth, and inheritance. You and you alone are my treasure, heart of my own heart, and my vision O ruler of all.

The next couple of years would be spent preparing for full time ministry. We set our vision toward what he now had confirmed through many experiences working in Mexico with unreached peoples. After investigation into several alternatives, we decided to form our own non-profit organization. We called it Scriptures in Use. The name was rooted in our desire to see the Scriptures used and applied to the lives of forgotten peoples. It was to be a much bigger undertaking, a bigger vision than I or anyone else imagined.

We started by raising personal support with our friends and church and launched out into full time ministry. Pastor Dan Gill held a special dedication to formally recognize what God had done in our lives over the past few years. It was during this time of dedication on June 7, 1987 that God had a word of prophesy for us.

Dan said, "The Lord has called you to something that is a lot bigger than what it looks like right now. The Father's vision is a vision for the whole world. He gave his Son that the whole world might have life if they would just believe in Him. And the Lord says that He's laid a country before you and a job before you that has never been done. The word of the Lord is: "Don't limit your vision to what you alone can accomplish- I believe the Lord is going to bring out of this something bigger, vaster, broader than you ever dreamed." So, the Lord says: "Don't limit your vision. Let your vision go, let it soar and in His way and in His own time God will bring it to pass-because there is more here at stake than one tribe. There's a nationwide work, and even a worldwide work that will come out of this."

Dan ended it by saying: "It is comforting that in Acts 13 when they sent those guys off, they prayed for them, laid hands on them and sent them away." Dan called for the elders to lay hands on Carla and me.

Then, our dear friend Jan Galindo got up and came to the front to share several verses with us. From Psalm 2:

"You are my son, today I have become your Father. Ask of me, and I will give the nations your inheritance, the ends of the earth your possession."

From Isaiah 54

> *"You will be far from oppression, for you will not fear the terror for it will not come near you. If anyone does attack you, it will not be my doing. Whoever attacks you will surrender to you. No weapon that is forged against you will prevail, and every tongue that accuses you in judgment you will condemn. This is the heritage of the servants of the Lord, and their vindication is from me, declares the Lord."*

Again, the Lord was speaking to Carla and me directly. The full force of these amazing prophesies made a lasting impression on us. I cried like a baby; I felt God's love pouring over me. I knew at that moment that God heard all my cries, and he answered in such a powerful way. He had planted me by streams of water and this was confirmation that I would be fruitful, and whatever Carla and I accomplished would prosper and grow. I knew it was my destiny to fulfill these promises given. He had given me words that were so personal, so encouraging, so uplifting. The church was confirming the vision God had given. Our vision was God's vision. He was sending us out with His authority, His anointing, and His power. My father would give us the nations and the ends of the earth. This would prove to be true, as time would tell.

Along with a great vision came God's provision. Our combined salaries from our professions in 1987 were more than enough to maintain the *"American Dream"*. However instead of following an affluent lifestyle, we instead had been saving enough to pay off our mortgage, get a truck and save for the lean years. "No debt" was a value we both believed in. When the moment came when God would send us out, we were prepared. *The*

American Dream is an illusion. Credit card and or even mortgage debt drives most people in America. When you get to your goal a new "want" is in sight off in the distant horizon. No matter how much money you make, there will be new ways to stay in debt to material things. Debt means not being free to serve the Lord. "*Let no debt remain outstanding, except the debt to love one another, for whoever loves others has fulfilled the law.*" *(Romans 13:8)* We decided to be servants depending on God for everything. Deciding to forego secure salaries like we were used to was only part of the sacrifice. We were going to war and wartime meant sacrifices. I tendered my resignation at the Star and Citizen and Carla gave notice at the school district too. The summer of 1987 I remember rejoicing in the Lord, "Free at last, free at last, thank God we are free at last." Another song rang in my heart:

> *Great is Thy faithfulness*
> *Great is Thy faithfulness*
> *Morning by morning new mercies I see*
> *And all I have needed Thy hand hath provided*
> *Great is Thy faithfulness*
> *Lord unto me*

The Lord is faithful in everything, even when we are not. But how difficult is it to trust Him when our future is at stake? Survival of the fittest is a part of our society. We see a bumper sticker that says, "The one who dies with the most toys wins." The unspoken pressures of living out the so-called American Dream were real and yet illusive. We decided that our lifestyle would be different. We would live out God's Dream, believing Him in all things. God had led us this far and he would not abandon us now. Carla and I trusted Him for the faith that he would provide adequately. *"Which of you fathers, if your son asks for a fish, will give him a snake instead?" (Luke 11:11)* We were asking and believing God for more than a fish. We were asking him to take care of us for a lifetime.

We were and are together in this. After over forty years of marriage, God continues to provide. Living the American Dream is not what Jesus taught us. Instead Jesus and the Holy Spirit were teaching us to live out what some people might call "Radical Christianity". Jesus was showing us how to live out the "Jesus People Dream." It meant to turn the world upside down. It meant living out His values. It meant living the Upside Down Life.

The Beatitudes are Jesus' most eloquent vision of this life. The Beatitudes present an upside down view of life. "The Message" puts it all in perspective and says it best. Matthew 5:3-16: *"Blessed are you when you're at the end of your rope. With less of you there is more of God. You're blessed when you feel you've lost what is most dear to you. You are blessed when you're content with just who you are-no more, no less. That's the moment you find yourselves proud owners of everything that can't be bought. You are blessed when you've worked up a good appetite for God. He's food and drink and the best meal you'll ever have. You're blessed when you care. At the moment of being "care-full", you find yourselves cared for. You are blessed when you get your inside world-your mind and heart-put right. Then you can see God in the outside world.*

You're blessed when you can show people how to cooperate instead of compete or fight. That's when you discover who you really are, and your place in God's family. You are blessed when your commitment to God provokes persecution. The persecution drives you even deeper into God's kingdom. Not only that-count yourselves blessed every time people put you down or throw you out or speak lies about you to discredit me. What it means is that the truth is too close for comfort and they are uncomfortable. You can be glad when that happens-give a cheer, even! – For though they don't like it, I do! All heaven applauds. And know that you are in good company. My prophets and witnesses have always gotten into this kind of trouble. Let me tell you why you are here. If you lose you saltiness, how will people taste God-flavors of this earth? You've lost your usefulness and will end up in the garbage.

Here's another way to put it: You're here to be light, bringing out the God-colors in the world. God is not a secret to be kept. We're going public with this, as public as a city on a hill. If I make you light-bearers, you don't think I'm going to hide you under a bucket, do you? I'm putting you on a light stand-shine! Keep open house; be generous with your lives. By opening up to others, you'll prompt people to open up with God, the generous Father in heaven."

Carla and I were going to the villages to share God's goodness, to be salt and light. God was not a secret to be kept. It was this message of salt and light that brought me to become a radical for Jesus. I could not hide it any more. I wanted to be light in a dark world, to minister to the hopeless, the despairing, and the poor. We wanted to do this in a way that all eyes were on Jesus and not on us.

The words were finally coming to pass that Jesus spoke a long time ago at the Billy Graham Crusade, "You are a soldier in the army of the Lord". This could happen only if I followed Him as my commander in chief into the "Upside Down" life, into life as his witness to the poor and disadvantaged of this world. Why?

Because the poor understand his message better that those with all the advantages. The poor understand they are in need of help and redemption; the poor have no exaggerated sense of their own importance. The poor expect little from competition and much from cooperation. The poor can distinguish between necessities and luxuries. The poor have little of this world to lose, and much to gain in the world to come.

19

Mexico, an Ocean of Needs

By the summer of 1987 we had sold our home in Tucson and bought an old house in Bisbee, Arizona near the border. It would serve as both a gateway to Mexico as well as a place of refuge. Bisbee was a small town in the southeast corner of the state with a Mexican border crossing at the little town of Naco, Sonora. We bought a truck and a camper that we would use for many years to travel in and out of Mexico. We traveled to many of the indigenous people groups and every trip had its own adventures. Our non-profit, tax-exempt organization Scriptures in Use was denominationally unaffiliated. Today, as then, it operates under a Board of Directors and advisors of pastors, missionaries, teachers and businessmen. Gary and Nancy Lovelace joined us as our very first board members and advisors back in 1987. Perhaps influenced by Wycliffe/SIL's experience-being asked to leave Mexico-we felt it would be best to have a low profile ministry.

Men and women of oral tradition don't have the habit of

reading or writing. Many hear the gospel as it is told to them in oral forms. As one Native American Indian has said, "Ours is an oral tradition. It can be heard in the way we think and speak. An oral tradition schools the memory and makes the spoken word a poem. Stories are a treasure of oral tradition, passed on in eloquence." We weren't sure exactly how to discover the best way to communicate to those of oral tradition, but we wanted to experiment with a variety of new methods.

We wrote to our prayer partners in June and July of 1987. "We are devoting our time completely to the goal of Scriptures in Use among unreached, indigenous people groups of Mexico. We desire to see the Scriptures become an integral part of the lives of believers and the unreached oral peoples in many tribal groups." We went on to say in our early communication, "We hope to teach the indigenous people how to read the Scriptures and understand them through discipleship training." We wanted to build bridges toward Christ. We wanted to experiment with a new approach of oral communication of the Scriptures. This approach many years later would develop into an important breakthrough in the modern mission's movement.

This was a tall order since most people groups were unaware of the translated Scripture that had been made available, especially since SIL was only a translation organization and did not have the goal of Scripture engagement. That goal would be left to others. In the summer of 1990 we were invited by the American Bible Society and Wycliffe Bible Translators to attend a conference in England to share our experiences with Scripture engagement in Mexico. It was another opportunity to learn from others, as there were many translators from many parts of the world attending. We spent over ten days sharing academic papers and personal experience from various perspectives and points of view. My paper was entitled *"Building Bridges for Scripture Use Among Oral Societies."* The question that always seemed to be on our minds was: "What is the most effective means to communicate the truths we find written in the Scriptures to an oral society?" I said to the group of translators. "The message is eternal, but cultural barriers and rapid change separate us. How can we build bridges of communication that lead to discovery? This often means a spoken message to people who have a long tradition of oral means of communication. Finding creative means of presenting the Scriptures orally without disturbing the accuracy of the message remains our greatest challenge."

We take for granted translated Scripture. It is everywhere and at a low cost. After all, one can buy a Bible at Wal-Mart and it is accessible to all. But we learned during the ten years from 1987 to 1997 that for many indigenous people, Scripture in their language was not available because it hadn't been translated or they couldn't read it. This was widespread. They also were not aware of the benefits of the Scriptures if they had been translated. On top of that many didn't think it was necessary to learn to read. It represented a big challenge, a God size challenge. It seemed like God was saying, "Start with training the leaders to communicate my message." We frankly were surprised. We didn't have the academic training so how were we to do this? We only had the Scriptures themselves, the Holy Spirit and common sense. We relied on what we learned in John 15:16 "You did not choose me, but I chose you to go and bear fruit, fruit that will last. Then the Father will give you whatever you ask in my name." Armed with the Scriptures and the Father's promise, we continued in Mexico where God had established our work.

We who live in the U.S.A. today also live in a society where many families do not read the Bible together nor have devotions as a family. There is a famine of the Word of God even among Christian families. Biblical literacy in America is at an all time low. "Scripture is the life blood of every believer." Jesus said to the unbelievers of his time *"You are in error because you do not know the Scriptures or the power of God." Matt 22:29*. Over and over Jesus asks one question: "What do the Scriptures say?" How could the poor and disadvantaged possibly know and understand the Scriptures. What is the goal of Scripture other than changed lives? God would make *himself* responsible to accomplish that big task. Get that. He would be responsible for the task ahead. I just had to trust Him enough to see it to completion. We had been transformed by God's wisdom; therefore people from unreached groups could be transformed too by Scripture and the Holy Spirit's guidance.

Over those ten years in Mexico, we held literacy workshops and completed Jesus Film projects among many tribal groups. There were lots of trials and tribulations throughout that season of our life. Carla had learned that literacy though viable for oral peoples was only taking hold among a small minority and she longed to use methods that fit with the oral, traditional learning styles we had observed in the villages. Together we decided to change her role and mine to curriculum writers, developing materials for leaders and indigenous pastors to establish a strategy of oral communication of the Scriptures in their mother tongue. We continued to record Jesus Film translations and Scripture Stories, to train leaders, mobilize workers among indigenous people, and mentor local pastors in several indigenous regions.

Carla and I ended that decade utterly exhausted from a physical point of view. At the same time we were energized in a spiritual sense. We had learned a great deal more about Scripture engagement, teaching the local people to use cultural strategies to present the Word of God. We had mentored leaders from over twenty language groups. Our team had grown over ten years. We had translated/recorded the Jesus Film in over fifty indigenous languages from many parts of Latin America. Nearing the end of a decade in the field we needed a break and our Board approved a sabbatical so we prayed and asked God for direction once again.

20

International Ministry

In 1996 the answer came when I met Phill Butler of an organization called "Interdev" based in the Seattle area. I met Phill at a Panama conference for indigenous pastors and leaders from all over Latin America. He was a speaker at the conference and he gave a presentation on cooperation and partnership. The subject was "Strategic Evangelism Partnerships for the 10/40 Window." We realized that our task was too big to do alone. We needed to learn partnership principles to develop the projects we had started in Mexico to achieve the multiplication results that were needed. Moving from small groups of believers to movements required partnership. There was a missionary movement beginning in Latin America. Young missionaries were catching the vision to go to the entire world. Because Latin American churches didn't have the resources like North American churches, the only way to accomplish this was through cooperation and partnerships. It was a movement that I wanted to be a part of. Phill specialized in training leaders from around the world to co-operate and to form partnerships where there was common ground. He had a lot of experience with this field and it was compelling and held great interest to me. I talked to Phill about the possibilities of taking a sabbatical internship with him and his organization. I explained to him that our board had approved a sabbatical of about nine months to a year. The Holy Spirit again was leading me.

He and his entire staff of ten welcomed me whole-heartedly to their Edmonds, Washington office. I started on January 2, 1996 and was assigned to be part of the team of people teaching partnership principles to leaders in India. Carla would stay in Seattle and go back to teaching for the school year. My first assignment at Interdev was to join a team of four going to Hyderabad, India for a training event that had been in the planning stages for some time. Since I had no experience, I would go as an observer. I was to take careful notes and learn the pacing of classes and structure of the partnership principles that were taught in India. They planned two events, one for Hyderabad, and the other in Delhi, each lasting ten days.

My Missionary Journal, January 25, 1996

At last we arrived and began adjusting to our new surroundings in Secunderabad-a small town on the outskirts of Hyderabad. We left Seattle on Monday and did not arrive in Delhi until 10:30 P.M. on Tuesday. Paul Miller and I have been enjoying our time together. As we traveled we talked of his many experiences in India and with Interdev. God is so good to me. He has blessed me through so many rich opportunities and India was just one more. Upon our arrival in Delhi, we bartered our way into a taxi and checked into the Centaur Hotel. Leaving Seattle on a nippy, icy January day and arriving into the musty, humid warmth of Delhi was a pleasant change. I was beginning to tire of the rain and sleet of Seattle. We left Delhi the following morning on an early flight to Hyderabad. The airport was abuzz with activity at 5:00 AM upon our arrival. Sikhs stood out with their turbans and well manicured beards. Classic faces were impressive, so were baggy pants tightly fitted at the bottom. The women of India were very beautiful with their long, flowing saris reflecting elegance uncommon to my homeland. One can't help notice the large variety of "dots" on the foreheads of so many. Some were bright red, others with a yellow circle around the red dot.

India was more modern than I expected, though it compared to Mexico in many ways, especially to Oaxaca and Chiapas because of the large mixture of tribal faces standing in stark contrast to the city people. Our arrival at the venue "Operation Mobilization" (O.M. for short) Center was uneventful. We settled into our rooms and right away I took off to explore the sights and sounds of India. O.M. was the central clearing house for most Christian literature in India where Christians represented a small minority. It was also the main training facility for all Indian O.M. workers and missionaries coming from India or a nearby country. The walk down the busy Nagpur Highway leading to Jedimetla village was the highlight of the day. I came upon a Hindu Temple in the final stages of construction. The teardrop dome was carved with many idols and demons. It was a very elaborate design typical of pictures I'd seen in National Geographic magazine. I photographed several views of the temple. A woman stood nearby. I suppose she was suspicious of my intentions. I waved to her and her husband as I left, wondering what they were thinking about the foreigner.

I walked further along the road passing a few "sacred cows," the first I had seen. Turning the corner I passed on to a small dirt road leading to a little village. As I passed through, I realized that I was nearing another Hindu temple; they seem to be on every corner. This time many people were worshiping. A haunting lonely chant rang out over the loud speaker. Many people were pacing back and forth, their heads bobbing as they chanted. I prayed as I walked. As I went on, I saw a man plowing his rice field with his oxen. A new village came into sight, women drawing water at the well, children running to see the "white" stranger. The architecture often reminded me of Mexico. I saw simple adobe houses with stucco. I saw wonderful bright colors standing out in a harsh and dry land.

I stopped briefly to exchange greetings with the locals. Few knew English and Telegu was their mother tongue. Coming to a large house with a big tree in front I noticed a young man with his baby daughter in his arms. I smiled and pulled out my Polaroid camera and took his picture. I held it out toward him to observe the photo appearing instantly before his eyes. He was glowing. Many family members rushed up to see the picture of their baby sister. We struggled to communicate, but then a young man appeared who spoke broken English, enough to invite me down the street to his brother's tent-making shop for tea. I gladly accepted and while chai was served they asked lots of questions. I began a geography lesson explaining I came from in the U.S.A. Where did I live? What was it like? Where is Washington? New York? We exchanged addresses. A customer arrived to rent a tent for a wedding function. Soon, we said our good-byes and I returned to the O.M. grounds. It was a nice adventure and I looked forward to more.

Our time at Hyderabad O.M. center was excellent. I learned about many rural and urban ministries that were collaborating together. I was deeply moved by the collective impact demonstrated as each shared his/her vision for ministry in different parts of urban Bombay,

Calcutta, Delhi, Madras, Púne, Gujarat, and Hyderabad. Jackie Pullenger, author of the book "Chasing the Dragon" had a very inspiring message. She shared her experiences in "the walled city" of Hong Kong during the past ten years. Her book gave a detailed account of her life inside the walled city filled with prostitutes, drug addicts, and gang leaders. Her message: Live among the people, love them, care for them, and be willing to be used, betrayed, to suffer, and share your possessions. Then God will change, renew, restore and save. I was moved and started praying.

I met a number of people from all parts of the world. I met and became friends with Jonathan Fletcher- pastor of an independent Anglican Church in Wimbledon U.K., Raju Abraham of Delhi, and Rolly Lamkang a young student from Nagaland near Burma. Rolly became very special to me. His English was quite good. He became our guide and we piled into a special motorized "rickshaw" call a "tuk tuk". This one was motorized but I saw many that were pulling the rickshaw by hand or by bicycle. Everywhere were human beasts of burden. They filled the streets along with thousands upon thousands of people creating a picture of liquid humanity oozing and flowing through the walkways, streets and shops. I was struck by the amazing skill of the drivers weaving in and out of traffic, avoiding pedestrians who jay walked at no small risk.

Rolly and Jonathan negotiated with the motor rickshaw driver to get us to our next destinations. Off we went to what seemed to me like Mr. Toad's Wild Ride. We moved out into dense traffic. We moved in and out of traffic skillfully once more right through major traffic jams. Distinctive remnants of the old capital of the Mogul Empire were showcased on ancient, narrow streets. They were omnipresent. Islamic and Arabian architecture was ubiquitous. We stopped for a while at the "Charminar Archway", towering high above the multitudes bustling through the city. It was built in 1591. I learned there that India had one of the largest Islamic populations in the world with over one hundred seventy five million people who revere Mohammed. I saw lots of women dressed in black with silky veils covering their faces. It was a Friday of Ramadan in which people fasted throughout the Islamic world. We then walked down a crowded street to Birla Temple.

It was there that I experienced a strange and unusual sensation. Birla Temple was a Hindu Temple where hundreds of gods were worshiped. It stood shrouded in brilliant white marble towering above Hyderabad. It reminded me of that day long ago when I stood at the Hindu Temple of Paramahansa in the U.S.A. and a clear voice rang out of the darkness into the light. I was thankful that Jesus had brought me so far from that world of deception. Upon arrival at Birla Temple everyone deposited his or her shoes in a locker room. There were many security guards all around ensuring compliance with all the rules of the temple. No bags or articles could be carried inside the temple.

Soon I ascended a large flight of stairs in a long line of Hindu worshipers. The marble walkway ascended to the third floor with a spectacular view. By now the monotone chanting by the young Hindu priests filled the air while the masses were pressing in. I passed by the place where the priests were perched in a nave. A young couple moved in close to receive a blessing from two priests with shaven heads and red-yellow robes. Their eyes were glowing and darting back and forth as though possessed with demons from hell. The chanting became louder and louder. We continued our journey single file and all around the perimeter of the third tier-by now one could sense the thick spiritual dark of night. I felt it clearly, this dominion of evil and deception. I started to pray in an unknown language. I prayed also as we circled the temple single file. As I passed I said in a low voice, "God, bring light to India!" I passed by various shrines and I noted how many dipped their hands into sacred water containers, perhaps as a symbol of cleansing akin to the washing in the River Ganges.

I finally returned to the exit deeply saddened. The verse came to me taken from John 1:5 "The light shines in the darkness, but the darkness has not understood it." The Gospel first came to India in the 17th century and India did not understand it. The shopkeepers were now crowded together as we made our way home. The god "Shiva" seemed to be everywhere. My short adventure was coming to a close. Pastor Jonathan was leaving the next day for Madras. I was grateful for his company and that of Rolly. Our partnership-training course drew together men and women from the southern part of India. From as far away as Trivandrum, Kerala, Madras, Bangalore, Bombay, and Pune they came. Our ten days together were very special and memorable. I was the partnership "tutor" for a group of five. Rolly Lamkang from Nagaland, Manipur province, Prem James from Bangalore, Rev. Bhagvanraj from Bombay, Prabharhr a Tamil working in the slums of Bangalore, and Satish Kumal working among the tribal youth. Also attending the course were PS Kuman and Sam Lovelson both working with Far Eastern Broadcasting Association of India. (FEBA) It occurred to me how many people from diverse backgrounds have given their life to the Lord. As a group we were working together to do problem solving, answer questions and write a partnership project for the course. We were knit together by God's grace as we prayed together at the end of the day's teaching, lectures, and study.

Rolly became my adopted son. He had now been away from his family in Manipur for more than four years. O.M. had given him training in many aspects of ministry. This course was his last before returning home to Manipur. One day, as dusk fell on Secunderabad, Rolly and I went for a long walk. As we talked, he shared with me that back home in Manipur, rebel insurgents had burned his village. Many were forced to join their cause or face immediate execution. Rolly's parents had escaped however; they were living in a small thatched house in the mountains where the Nagas fled. Now it was time for Rolly to return home. He was of course very fearful and concerned about his parents and his own safety in passing through occupied rebel territory. There had been reports of Naga people taken off the buses and executed on the spot. Rolly was a young man of twenty-five years. He had done well in school; his written skills in English were very good. I could see that from his class work. We talked a long while and then prayed together for him, his family, and his long journey from Hyderabad to Manipur.

Saturday, we concluded our training course with prayer and a communion service. Our last day was memorable. I took the bus into town with some of the brothers who were returning home. They were headed for the train station. I was so excited to see the historic railway system built and dominated for so long by the British. It was reminiscent of the days of the Raj. A train was just arriving. I loved the sounds of the train station. I heard the inscrutable announcements on the loud speaker and the steam rushing from the locomotive and those wonderful faces of every description. All those incredible faces! I strolled about the station soaking in the marvelous experience. It was hot and humid. I could only imagine this place in summer.

India is rich in color and beauty. Overall they seemed a polite people and happy to be photographed. The faces of children especially moved me with their eyes so bright and filled with hope and joy.

Though they were poor in this world's goods, they were rich in spirit. Soon, two teenage boys I met and photographed at a teashop showed up on their motorbikes. "Where are you going?" they asked. "Just down the street to find another photograph," I said. "Come with us. We are going to school, you will find many photographs there." I climbed on the back of their bike and off we went. I wondered if they were telling the truth. It turned out that they were students at Loyola College of India, a very famous Catholic School. The Lord always has my back. The function turned out to be an Indian performing arts festival. We arrived to the sight of a large and very colorful Arabian style tent. Several hundred students were seated, behaving very politely and all very well dressed. As I approached, the act on stage was a mime act, followed by a girl singing traditional Indian Karnataka. Next, two boys played classic Karnataka with violin, sitar, and tabla drum. The highlight of the afternoon was six girls from Rajasthan. Their dresses and headwear were stunning in bright reds and greens. They moved together in perfect unison to the exotic and unfamiliar music.

It was now time to leave Secunderabad and all our new friends at O.M. We boarded our plane for Delhi and in only two hours we arrived safely. I had lots of laughs with Paul Miller who can make a joke about most anything. His influence was very welcomed. "His was a merry heart that did good like a medicine."

Sunday, we taxied across town to Bible Bahvan. It happened that the founding missionary who had returned to Ireland was speaking today. He was Robert Duff from Belfast. He had been in India for over 40 years and had only recently returned after having quadruple bypass surgery in Ireland. His years of service had produced a fine short term Bible School- he called it a "Youth Ashram". It occurred to me that wouldn't it be wonderful if Carla and I could provide short-term training for young men and women of India. It was a fleeting idea that I tucked away in my heart.

After the worship services at Bible Bahvan, Dr. Raju Abraham took us to our rooms at the Indian Social Institute (ISI). We were now staying in the heart of Delhi's diplomatic service quarter. There was a strange contrast all around us. The streets were lined with beautiful trees with well-manicured green grass lining the majestic buildings of the quarter. However, squatters have moved in all around the diplomatic quarter. They built little houses of cardboard, plastic, broken bricks and discarded pieces of wood. Their poverty was painful.

As I looked around, I saw tall buildings filled with important people-diplomats and bureaucrats. In stark contrast, I saw the poor of Delhi, the slum people, the lame, the sick, and the blind, all so desperately poor. It was also a reminder of the special place that Jesus has for the poor. "Come to me all you who are heavy laden and I will give you rest." Those images would stick with me for many years to come.

21

Discipleship Through Storytelling

Those better informed than I say it is believed that in the 1st Century the Apostle Thomas went to preach the Gospel in India and that Thomas founded the church in the South of India. It remains strong to this day. Today, there are about fifty-five million Christians in India. About half are Protestants and half are Roman Catholic. They are a small minority among India's over one billion population.

The partnership course here in Delhi has gone extremely well. The leadership here is of very high quality. The goal of this training was to formalize plans to train two hundred trainers in Strategic Evangelism Partnerships in order to multiply the trainers and workers on the ground. Dr. Raju Abraham the leader of this group had attracted many doctors and heads of Indian hospitals to the meetings. Also, many leaders of Indian mission agencies and various heads of para-church organizations were also in attendance. The long term goal of this group was to mobilize and train fifty thousand (50,000) grass roots church planters from throughout India who work in the regions of Manipur, Bihar, Uttar Pradesh, Rajasthan, Punjab, Jammu-Kashmir and other states. It would be called the North India Harvest Network. The organization in turn had member agencies working in Bhutan, Pakistan and Afghanistan.

I shared with a small working group about our new course for oral learners called Discipleship Through Storytelling (DST). It consisted of a storyteller's guide based on seven principles of discipleship obedience that Jesus taught and presented through Biblical stories. "Our experience with the Jesus Film was good", I said to the group, "but follow up and making disciples after the Jesus Film was a big challenge because so many could not read or write." I told them we wanted something that oral learners could understand. In order to achieve that, we had developed a simple course that taught Repentance through the story of Jesus and Zacchaeus and Baptism through the story of Philip and the Ethiopian. We taught Love of God and your Neighbor through the story of the Good Samaritan. They learned to practice the Lord's Supper though the story of the Lord's Supper. Prayer was taught through the story Jesus Teaches us to Pray. We taught about Giving through the story of the Poor Widow. They learned to Share their faith with others from the Great Commission story of Matthew 28:16-20. I told them that Carla and I had been experimenting with this different approach to follow up and discipleship after showing the Jesus Film. This was an approach that was new to everyone in the room even though these simple stories were available to all. Everyone could tell the story whether he/she could read or not. After the story, the new believers could participate actively through specific dialogue questions. The stories of the Bible illustrated truth for ordinary people in an easy to understand narrative. Our field tests showed that it was a non-threatening way to share the Gospel. It was the first real breakthrough we had in Mexico and I told them I wanted to test it in India.

After a time of evaluating the course manual, the leadership decided to experiment with DST as part of their strategy for India's large populations of oral learners. They would use it on a trial basis and evaluate it afterward. I was very excited about this development. I met with several people who were interested in knowing more about it. I met a couple from Bihar, India, Sheila and Srinivasan Devasahayam Ponraj. They were missionaries sent out by the church in the south. The Church of North India and the Evangelical Church of India ordained him. We struck up a conversation and seemed to immediately feel a God-given connection. I explained that I worked in Mexico with tribal peoples and both Sheila and Ponraj said they were working in the state of Bihar, a poor and remote part of Northern India. They were working among tribal people as well. We shared many problems that we held in common. We exchanged contact information and said our goodbyes. This was a moment of destiny, a connection that we were praying for. The North India Partnership would play a big role in extending the Kingdom of God to oral peoples. I didn't know it then, but God would use DST and storytelling as major means to reach people of oral tradition that would not be otherwise reached.

As I had attended the partnership training I realized that India was a complex mosaic of many different castes, thousands of languages and dialects, each with a diverse set of challenges. It seemed overwhelming. I was glad that God had made himself responsible for India. I just followed His lead.

At mid-day breaks, I took off to see some of the sights of Delhi. I got into an auto-rickshaw and we took off along the streets of New Delhi built by the British. The streets were extremely wide and well kept. On the way, I could see the large Parliament building in the distance. I passed through a flurry of traffic whizzing by. From the backseat of the *"Tuk-tuk"*, my imagination carried me away to days past when India was still a "jewel in the crown" of the colonial empire. Except for a few modern cars the sights, sounds and smells of Delhi and its many faces continued to fascinate. I saw the faces of Burma, Nepal, China, Bhutan, Kashmir and Afghanistan. The border of China was less than two hundred and fifty miles northeast of Delhi, Nepal less than two hundred miles, and Pakistan less than two hundred and fifty miles west. India seemed like the center of the eastern world with all its great diversity and complexity.

I met with Dr. Victor Choudhrie the last night I spent in Delhi at the Centaur Hotel. We struck up a friendship during my video interview with him on Friday afternoon at Bible Bhavan. We had dinner together near the Delhi Airport. He would have liked to recruit me to become the International People Group advocate for the Gond tribe in Madhya Pradesh, which is in the central part of India. No lack of jobs to do in the Kingdom of God. We were on the next flight to the U.K. where the staff of Interdev was to meet for strategic planning. The time I had in India had been superb. I only wish that Carla could have been there to share this with me.

In no time at all our nine months of sabbatical was at an end. I learned so much about unreached peoples. The key partnership lesson was simple, "relationships of trust." God kept repeating this to me. God had set me apart through a personal relationship, trusting Jesus. That meant a relationship in which God talks to me and to everyone in an attitude of trust. But the missing piece for me, personally, was this: God wanted me to take another step, to learn to trust my brothers completely. That was hard. I had not learned that lesson well. I held back from my brothers and sisters in Christ, I trusted in myself too much. It's one thing to trust God; it's another to trust your brother. Jesus gently led me to trust others, little by little. We are made in his image and likeness to live in relationship with one another and with Him. He is our way maker. If we follow His lead he will make a highway in the wilderness. Along a dimly lit road, he makes everything bright and clear. I wanted to learn that hard lesson and I was determined that this was what God wanted of me. I offered up this prayer: "Lord, let me learn of the riches of following you. Guide me to follow you in the way of wisdom, lead me along the straight path."

God was doing so much around the world yet there was still so much remaining to be done. The growth in the number of missionaries being sent out by the Developing World churches was phenomenal. He was confirming my desire to see a multiplication of workers. We would see our growth come from the harvest itself. In India, the number of missionaries grew from 148 in 1963 to 4,391 in 1988. More than ten years ago, the number was 44,000 missionaries from 440 agencies and getting bigger every day. In Korea, they sent out 160 in 1984, 4321 in 1993 and in 2006 over 12,000 missionaries representing 166 agencies. In Africa: Kenya 673 missionaries from 53 agencies, Nigeria 3,800 from 150 agencies. Brazil, 4,754 full time workers from 132 agencies. Pakistan, 74 missionaries from 15 agencies (Source Operation World 6th edition updated and revised 2006) While these figures have not been updated in a while, the trend was clear. At a meeting I attended in Panama, Latin America 250 mission leaders were planning to send thousands of missionaries through strategic evangelism partnerships. The church overseas has experienced unprecedented growth. Working within this context, God was demonstrating to me the value of training huge numbers of national missionaries and lay people around the world to communicate the Scriptures to oral peoples. *"So, Paul left them. He took the disciples with him and had discussions daily in the lecture hall of Tyrannus. This went on for two years, so that all the Jews and Greeks who lived in the province of Asia heard the word of the Lord." Acts 19:9-10.*

We began a new but ancient model for ministry sending out missionaries two by two, to train those in the Third World in the manner prescribed in Acts 19. We would go to them. Carla and I and our team would train missionaries in the villages.

22

Communication Bridges

"He put a new song in my mouth, a hymn of praise to our God. Many will see and fear the Lord and put their trust in him."

Psalm 40:3

God had been at our side, leading, guiding and making a difference in our work for ten years. We had reached several milestones during that time. We had completed fifty translations/dubbings of the Jesus Film. At the same time Campus Crusade had completed their 400th Jesus Film. Wycliffe/SIL, with publishers like the Bible League had now completed two thousand translations of the New Testament. Making Scripture available whether in the form of a printed Bible or in the form of the Jesus Film and Scripture recordings was a significant team effort and achievement. It was God's plan that each one would do his/her part, working together to make a difference, contending as one man for the faith of the Gospel.

With all the progress we had made, Carla and I knew that God still had so much more for us to discover about oral learners. Slowly we were beginning to unlock God's hidden treasure for oral peoples, but like so many times before there were still important pieces to the puzzle yet to be found. We prayed more intensely than ever. Where Oh Lord? Slowly, He began to make a clearing in the wilderness, to make a straight path to the goal.

We returned home to Bisbee in order to transition from Mexico to an International ministry during the next couple of years. 1996 was filled with activities both in Latin America and around the world. Carla and I still had ongoing ministry among the Tarahumara for follow up work. We were continuing a partnership with Alfredo Guerrero as leader of the Mexican Association *Mano Amiga* (Helping Hands), recruiting and sending new missionaries to the Tarahumara area. Alfredo also served as the President of COMIMEX, Mexico's network for mission sending agencies globally. We had also become very involved with the AD 2000 and Beyond movement. It was a network developed on the worldwide scale for reaching the unreached. We had been able to be a part of this movement with a special interest in reaching the oral peoples of the world in partnership with ministries like Gospel Recordings, Wycliffe/ SIL, Campus Crusade, Southern Baptists, Assemblies of God, CBN and others. It was an exciting time to be working together, to be part of a unified effort. Part of God's amazing plan of completing the Great Commission, was to not work independently or in competition with one another. We were truly blessed to be living out the new reality of partnership toward oral peoples.

By the fall of 1996 we were in Oaxaca again working on

several projects. We visited our old friends in Manzanito and other new friends among other groups like the Zapotecs, Mixes, Chinantecs, and Triques. We rented a small apartment in Oaxaca City and stayed through New Years of 1997. We worked hard writing a new training course, taking all that we had learned during the past ten years of fieldwork. We saw many growing in Jesus with our existing course called Discipleship Through Storytelling. The new course we were writing was called "Communication Bridges to Oral Cultures" and its completion was a milestone event. It became known as "Bridges" for short. We took the time to stop and think about all we had learned through various experiences in the field and put them down on paper. We had learned a lot. What were these bridges to communicating more effectively to oral learners? We thought them through carefully.

One by one, we identified ten Bridges or concepts that needed to be passed on to others. First of all, the people who were oral learners were the best suited to reach people of oral tradition. Nearly all of the pastors and leaders we had the privilege of working with were oral learners, but many of them had been to Bible Schools taught by book learners. They were semi-literate, meaning they had limited literacy and had great difficulty comprehending what they read. Limited comprehension meant confusion or lack of clarity. They learned literate methods designed to reach a literate society but their fieldwork was among the unschooled, oral communicators. We finally sorted it out by turning the learning process on its head. That is, we taught semi-literates as well as oral learners in the manner of Jesus, using the Parables and stories of the Bible and much more. Jesus, though he could read was an oral communicator. We believed evangelization occurred one story at a time, each story building on the next. Our target audiences were oral learners and stories were understood best through dialogue questions that were concrete, based on the actions of the characters in the story. That was an important break-through for us. Oral learners are most responsive to concrete questions. At first, Carla and I struggled to discover the best questions and how to formulate them. Finally, we studied the kind of questions Jesus asked. Most always they were concrete, simple questions.

The course was designed to point out the differences between two very different learning styles or methods, oral or liter-ate. Participants would learn in the first lesson that both oral and literate methods were valid. After all, the Bible itself en-courages both. One must choose an oral method or a literate method depending on whom you are teaching. In India, most people were oral learners; many were completely illiterate and some semi-literate. Research and over ten years of experience had taught us that two-thirds of the world was comprised of oral communicators. Why had we not learned this important lesson before? We also had discovered that literate church planters have more difficulty communicating with oral learners. Whether literate or oral we had to learn the skills to "bridge the gap". Other bridges we identified included the importance of the native language, the example of Jesus as storyteller, and Bible storytelling with concrete dialogue or conversation that helps each participant understand the story.

We had discovered that oral learners were excited to learn about the events of the Bible and that it held their attention. This was exciting for us. We included in the lessons the strat-egies to develop church planting teams, to follow a circular process of church planting, to tell God's story from Creation to Revelation. We stressed the importance of the parables of Jesus. We introduced the formation of disciples and leaders through storytelling and using cultural adaptions to Scripture in song and also drama. Those ten bridges encapsulated the basics of all we had learned. These Bridges would eventually become known throughout the world in ways we could not have imagined then. Bridges would become a tool by which thousands upon thousands would come to trust in Jesus and be discipled and matured in Christ. During the next twenty years our team would teach thousands of grass roots church planters. But, I'm getting ahead of myself; the full impact of that would not be known for a while. There was still so much work to do.

In our course we encouraged young believers to be story-tellers in every aspect of their life. In fact, their very identity became one of a storyteller instead of a preacher. From plowing their fields to selling at the market they could tell God's story. They could recite a Scripture narrative whenever they met with friends, neighbors or even strangers. We taught discovery Storytelling the Gospel could become a way of life. They could learn from their peers and mentors the art of telling stories to everyone around them.

With the completed course in hand, we decided to go back to India to test it and to make necessary changes. We traveled in January of 1998 and met up with our dear friends SD Ponraj and Sheila Ponraj. We had kept in close contact since we met in Delhi the year before. We had never been to Bihar before. It was known as the graveyard of missions. This sounded ominous and indeed daunting. Much effort, time, and money had been spent on reaching Bihar, with little success. But that didn't matter; we headed out for India because God had told us to go and to expect great things. It was such an exciting time in our life. The following notes from Carla's missionary journal perfectly describe our trip.

23

Night Train to Madhupur

From Carla's Missionary Journal January 18, 1998

Reaching the departing train in Patna is frightening, one of the most terrifying experiences of my life. Going in both directions the crowds are ruthless. I cling to Jim as we maneuver though the multitudes to the second-class compartments and finally we are herded into the wrong car. It is unlit, brooding, and unwelcoming. After what seems an eternity we are settled into our right seats, next to a stern, khaki clad policeman from Delhi, who soon disappears into a profound sleep. We are surrounded by men—trains seem largely a man's domain—who speak Hindi, Santali, Bengali, or Bhojpuri. The sounds of languages we do not understand, merge with the clattering and clanking of the train. Somber and gleaming eyes glare at us suspiciously in the darkness.

As we leave for Madhupur, I gather together my images and memories of Patna, the capital of Bihar state in Northeast India, where live the poorest of the poor and the most religious Hindus and

Buddhists. Visually, Patna is defined by the Ganges River and dirt streets lined with bicycle rickshaws, decorated with fabrics and gaudy jewels, hundreds of them always waiting, hoping for a rider. I could never have been prepared for Patna by any film or photo or book. One can only truly imagine India when one confronts India face to face. Then comes the reality of lives lived amidst the earth and dirt, surrounded by teaming hordes of others clamoring for their bit of the land.

All stereotypes of India merge in the streets of Patna. Infinite, brilliant colors of silks and woven fabrics, folded, twisted and tied into the shapes of millennia-old dress styles. Turbans, face coverings, shawls, scarves, saris and the rust, red-brown of the tunics of the Buddhist monks. Noises dominated by auto horns and mayhem. Smells…of sewage mingled with spices, frying foods, chai, cardamom, ginger, garlic, sweat and the stench of polluted humidity.

The train screeches to a standstill at remote, unlit, unmarked stations in tiny Bihari towns and uneasy nagging sets in. Our train will arrive in Madhupur at about 2:00 AM and we will have no idea we are there. No announcements, no signs, I recall then, the endless warnings about robberies and assaults and the destitution of Bihar that we have heard before even leaving Delhi. We begin to make known to anyone who will listen that we wish to de-board in Madhupur. Madhupur… the name resonates throughout the car. When the train slows down at the station at least five people kindly let us know we have arrived. We rush past the crowds asleep on the ground outside the station in the cold, winter morning. We make a phone call and after a cup of hot chai we are whisked off in an old jeep to the School of Tribal and Multi-Cultural Studies where we will teach. We are housed in a decrepit ruin of the British Raj where the East India Company employees once stayed when they left Calcutta for holidays.

We fall exhausted into bed knowing that once more God has taken us safely through a very hard and dark journey. His purposes are always more profound and eternal than we sense with our finite minds. The days ahead prove exhilarating and challenging as we begin training sessions with one hundred grass roots church planters, dedicated to Bihar's one hundred million people. "Those who sow in tears will reap with songs of joy. He who goes out weeping, carrying seed to sow, will return with songs of joy." Psalm 126:5,6

The next day we taught *"Communication Bridges to Oral Cultures"* to a large group of young and eager grass roots church planters with amazing success, not just because it was received by the local people so well, but also because it yielded such amazing results. For the next twenty years "Bridges" was taught to thousands and thousands who learned to effectively reach oral learners throughout India. I quote from a Lausanne Occasional Paper entitled *"Making Disciples of Oral Learners"*. This was the first conference to fully recognize the needs of the unreached masses of indigenous oral peoples. The conference was held in 2004 at the Lausanne Committee for World Evangelism held in Pattaya, Thailand September 29 through October 5. It was a milestone event that brought worldwide recognition to a growing orality movement.

In the first chapter of their paper they quote from an Indian pastor who attended a Bridges seminar held by Sheila and SD Ponraj in 1999.

"Pastor Dinanath of India tell his story of ministry among his people:

"I was saved from a Hindu family in 1995 through a cross-cultural

missionary. I had a desire to learn more about the word of God and I shared this with the missionary. The missionary sent me to Bible College in 1996. I finished my two years of theological study and came back to my village in 1998. I started sharing the good news in the way I learnt in Bible College. To my surprise my people were not able to understand my message. A few people accepted the Lord after much labor. I continued to preach the gospel, but there were little results. I was discouraged and confused and did not know what to do."

But then Pastor Dinanath's story takes a major turn: "In 1999 I attended a seminar where I learnt how to communicate the gospel using different oral methods. I understood the problem in my communication as I was mostly using a lecture method with printed books, which I learnt in the Bible school. After the seminar I went to the village but this time I changed my way of communication. I started using a storytelling method in my native language. I used gospel songs and the traditional music of my people. This time the people in the villages began to understand the gospel in a better way. As a result of it people began to come in large numbers. Many accepted Christ and took baptism. There was one church with few baptized members in 1999 when I attended the seminar. But now in 2004, in six years we have seventy-five churches with one thousand three hundred and fifty baptized members and one hundred more are ready for baptism."

The book goes on to say: "Ironically, an estimated 90% of the world's Christian workers presenting the gospel use highly literate communication styles. They use the printed page or expositional, analytical and logical presentations of God's word. This makes it difficult, if not impossible, for oral learners to hear and understand the message and communicate it to others."

India is one of the most needy places on earth. The most un-reached people groups are in India, there are 2,292 unreached groups of a total of 2,560 groups. The population is 1 billion three hundred million and growing fast. To give some perspective, the whole world has over 3 billion people still unreached. Quick math shows that nearly 1/3 of the unreached people of the whole world live in India. Nearly 25% of the world's population or nearly 2 billion have never heard the name of Jesus. These are statistics from Operation World that was last updated in 2006.

Following the Lausanne Committee on World Evangelism Conference held in Thailand a new network was launched, the International Orality Network (ION). Carla and I launched the Bridges Training Network of South Asia (BTNSA) in 2008. To this day, both networks along with others serve the body of Christ to train and identify the needs of oral peoples and to place resources and manpower where they are most needed. They are the product of working together toward a common goal: The Kingdom of God until He comes again.

Between 1998 and 2015 Carla and I traveled throughout the world presenting Bridges training. We were amazed that no matter where we went in the developing world among oral cultures the issues were the same. The same concerns and bridges of communication we had observed in Mexico during our fieldwork applied wherever we taught Bridges. The teams we recruited also traveled to teach. As the home-based team grew and national master trainers proliferated I spent more and more time administrating SIU and raising funds for the ever-expanding needs of the team. I greatly missed the field that had always been my passion-but God had also given me gifts of administration. I was able to use those gifts to develop and expand Internationally. By 2015 I was ready to prepare a new leader for a growing team and to pass the baton on to the next generation.

24

Celebration in India

Fast forward to January 29, 2015. Carla and I had been training national workers around the world, targeting unreached, oral peoples for more than thirty years. But for now we were on our way to India for the last time. There was a celebration being given in our honor. I was humbled and deeply touched that we would be recognized for nineteen years of service to India. The story of our return to Madhupur is a long one. I don't know where to begin. We have so many dear friends it would be like writing a book of epic proportions if we adequately chronicled all that happened in nearly twenty years. So, for now, it is enough to take up this story from here.

From My Missionary Journal

I was in my room at 4 A.M. in Madhupur, a small town in Northeastern India in what was now the state of Jharkhand. We left for India from Tucson on Sunday January 25th. The journey is still a long one just as it always has been. Arriving in Delhi on Monday late, at 11 P.M.

we spent a noise-filled, restless night with the din of teaming life and sounds of the city that never sleeps. Delhi is one of the most populated cities in the world with twenty million souls. One sees the signs of the modern twenty first century yet with clear evidence of an ancient lifestyle creating great contradictions.

We stayed the night at Les Season Hotel near the airport. Uneventful! Up early the next morning to catch our plane to Patna only to learn our flight was cancelled and every other flight was fully booked. We prayed. People in Madhupur were expecting us. Nearly one hundred leaders from all over India, Nepal and Burma were coming to say their goodbyes and to strategize for the future. A wonderful celebration had been planned. Finally, a miracle! We were able to secure seats on Jet Air business class to Patna in time to catch a night train leaving from Patna to Madhupur. It was a considerable challenge to procure tickets on the "night train to Madhupur". Thank you Jesus for making a way in the wilderness. Chandan and Pramila met us at the Patna Airport. They took us to their home and fed us while we got caught up on all the news of the brethren and churches in India. Chandan and Pramila were among our first students in India in 1999.

Our previously purchased train tickets were lost because we had missed our 3 P.M. connection in Patna. By God's amazing grace, our dear friend Daniel Kamaraj was traveling from Chandigarh to the same celebration. He was a good friend and co-worker in the gospel. He held a confirmed seat on the "night train to Madhupur". He gave up his sleeping berth and he stood for the five-hour journey, stopping at every small station along the way. By means of another small miracle, Chandan, Pramila, and Daniel were able to negotiate seats with the conductor obtaining seats when passengers got off the train, only to lose the seat again later when a new passenger got on wanting his confirmed seat. They call India a land where people have mastered the art of chaos, yet somehow, we arrived in Madhupur safely at 3 A.M. where were met by Daniel Ponraj. Daniel was in boarding school when we came to Bihar almost twenty years ago. Now he is a grown man serving the Lord with distinction. Once again, God brought us to the remote town of Madhupur on the same night train we took many years ago. Our return seemed like a dream.

Daniel Ponraj took us to Hotel Kumar International, the best hotel in town- in fact the only hotel in town. It had been built recently. We were all very glad to arrive there safely and sleep a few hours before opening ceremonies got started the next morning at 9 A.M. Daniel Ponraj officially called the 7th Annual Roundtable Consultation for the Bridges Training Network of South Asia to order with nearly one hundred leaders from all over South Asia arriving for this historic event. Carla and I saw so many brothers and sisters we loved-this time they were not strangers but rather old friends. SD Ponraj and his wife Sheila were there to greet us with great big smiles, hugs and kisses.

Over the years, we had met and instructed many young leaders working in diverse parts of India. There were in attendance people we had mentored for all these years, Babu Rau, Dr. Saheb and Rita, Rev. Francis, Dr. Abhi Sethia, Rev Chandan Sah, Nari Ram, Sanjay James, Dr. Eppan John, Daniel Kamaraj, and so many others in-cluding Dil Tamang who brought eighteen brothers and sisters from Nepal and Myanmar to wish us well upon our retirement and say farewell. The events of the 7th Annual Roundtable Consultation went by so quickly that before I knew it the farewell ceremonies were to begin on the evening of the 29th. Sheila Ponraj had planned an elaborate gala event with flowers that filled the room and a large banner that prominently read, "Thank You for Your Service to India". The Santali oral arts team took us by the hand to lead Carla and me into the conference hall. They stopped along the way to perform the traditional foot washing ceremony of the Santali tribe. Sheila dressed Carla and I with the finest clothing fit for a Maharaja and Maharani of Madhupur. They dressed us and treated us like royalty. It was very humbling even at times embarrassing. However, we were reminded by all of our Indian friends that it was "right and fitting" that they honor us in the "Indian Way."

Everyone came forward with his or her stories, memories of love, and affection. Dil and the Nepali's tribute were so powerful; there was hardly a dry eye in the audience. Each of the eighteen brothers and sisters came forward with a bright yellow or white scarf and placed it over our shoulders. Each passed by in "the Nepali Way" according to Dil. They said a blessing-then leaning forward placed the yellow scarf one on top of the other until all eighteen were piled over each of our shoulders. Then Dil read from the inscription on a special plaque that was presented to us. I will never forget their word of love and appreciation for the years we had worked together to see the Nepali church grow and mature.

Dr. SD Ponraj presented us with his new book "Developing Disciples and Leaders Among Oral Learners," a book about the principles and practices of effective communication. It was the result of the years he had spent testing and living out these principles in India. He presented a signed copy with a written dedication to Carla and me at the beginning of the book for all the years we worked together advancing the gospel among oral learners.

Later, I read a quote in the book by David Hesselgrave, one of the outstanding modern-day missiologists from the Western

Church. He made the following important comments about the present-day orality-literacy debate, *"Literacy and Bible Translation have been front and center in missionary theory and practice. At least one-third of the world's peoples are without a written language. That is still fewer than half of the known languages where oral communication is the only way to pass on information. It is the preferred form of learning and communication for many more. Taking all this into account, it is sometimes claimed that an emphasis on oral communication of the Scriptures may be the next great advance."*

The orality-literacy debate that David Hesselgrave talks about in his statement is important. The events in our return to Madhupur inspired many memories. After reflecting on my life, it seemed that God had graciously allowed Carla and me to join several early pioneers in the previously unexplored arena of oral communication of the Scriptures. This movement has now gone mainstream and been accepted by the larger missions movement and has even been adopted for use in the U.S.A. especially among the youth and immigrant populations. It took thirty years of fieldwork and direction from the Lord to work through the issues that confront oral learners. Jesus used Mexico and India in our lives in powerful ways. I was so thankful to God during that gala event in Madhupur.

The celebration coordinators took time to recognize Carla for her authorship of "Bridges for Women" and her contribution on behalf of the women of India. They made a large special banner that read: *"Dear Carla, You are very special to us. Thank you for making us a part of Bridges Network for Women. Love you Carla, God bless you and Jim."*

That was a night I will guard in my heart always. The elders of the Santali church came forward. Many years ago there were few believers among them-now there were dozens who were now ordained ministers and though they were "unschooled, ordinary men" they had demonstrated that they had been with Jesus. The Bridges leadership training for oral learners had changed everything. It was a proud moment for the Santali leaders and it was an unforgettable moment for Carla and me.

The next day the highlight was the Santali "Oral Arts Festival" that took place in Ruthwadi, the very same village where we filmed "The Ancient Path" nearly eighteen years ago. We saw many of the same believers that participated in the film. There were many more lovely moments and events. It is impossible to record the many blessings we received through so many brothers and sisters in India. I must thank the Lord Jesus Christ who made us one in Spirit. The Apostle Paul when he gave his farewell to the Ephesian church said- "I know that I will likely never see your faces again- but I am confident that one day we will meet again in heavenly places."

The evening ended with sixteen representatives performing Scripture stories in song and dance typical of the diversity of regions. There were also songs from Karnataka as well as Madhupur. As part of the celebration we were reintroduced to grassroots, non-literate church planters we knew in the late 90's who are now the leaders in the region. Santali tribal believers danced to the rhythm of the *dolak* and presented us with garlands.

It was end of the India road for me. Again, I thought back to Paramahansa Yogananda's words and that day in May 1974 when I gave my heart, not to Paramahansa, but to Jesus. That great day Jesus found me in a Hindu Temple and said, "What you are looking for you will not find here!" Instead, He called me to become "a soldier in the army of the Lord." He called me, an ordinary man, to take up my cross and follow Him to the ends of the earth. It was a unique path but an ancient path, one that had been traveled by many before me. The Holy Spirit is the great hound of heaven. He chased me down, finding me in a miserable state of mind and heart. He can do this for all who call on his name. He is the Alpha and Omega, the beginning and the end. He is the wind in my sails, the song I will be singing forever.

I conclude my memoir with this tribute to the Lord, to all He has done. This is a song by Matthew Ward in words that will live forever in my heart and have been an inspiration to me.

Knowing You

All I once held dear, built my life upon
All this world revers and wants to own
All I once thought gain, I have counted loss
Spent worthless now, compared to this
Knowing You Jesus, Knowing You
There is no greater thing
You're my all, you're the best
You're my Joy, my righteousness,
And I love you Lord.
Now, my desire is to know you more
To be found in you and known as yours
To possess by faith what I could not earn
All surpassing gift of righteousness

Knowing you Jesus, knowing you
There is no greater thing
You're my all, you're the best,
You're my joy my righteousness
And I love you Lord.

25

Final Reflections

This memoir was not meant to be a thorough treatment of my life but rather a record of my journey in search of a father, in search of purpose and meaning. I found this purpose and meaning in Jesus Christ who forever changed the course of my life.

As I reflect on my father and the events of his life I am reminded of the verse in Romans 2:15 when the apostle Paul says that God has written his law on our hearts and that our consciences also bear witness. My father was born into an unjust, corrupt world and he wanted justice. He justified stealing the Krupp Diamond because Alfried Krupp obtained it by corrupt and unjust means, being part of killing the Jews and enslaving millions and millions of people. My dad could see the injustice; his intensions were good, but his means of getting justice was corrupt. He said to me often, "stealing from corrupt people wasn't stealing at all". But this was not God's justice.

However seeking God's sense of justice instead of my dad's, led me to the years of the Jesus People Movement when I grew to love Him and love His Word. I followed my conscience and my heart. He took me to the uttermost parts of the world to make disciples and He used everything for His glory. He started whole movements in over thirty people groups of the world. I am so blessed and so very grateful that He interceded at pivotal moments along the way and called me to a lifetime of service. The vision we had in the early days for the poor and disadvantaged, for those without access to the Scriptures, has been passed on to the current staff of fourteen at Scriptures in Use and leader Kent Kiefer. They still advocate for traditional, oral people groups across the globe through training and empowerment and very importantly thousands of Bridges trainers have been raised up in the countries where SIU has introduced training. They continue to reproduce, inspire new workers, and multiply. Each new generation has built on the previous, but God and Christ the Messiah get all the glory. Believers have been trained from Nigeria to Burkina Faso and Cameroon, from all parts of Nepal to Assam in Northeast India, to Myanmar and Bhutan. We have trained many in Central Asia, in Pakistan, and Kashmir, in the Middle East countries of Syria, Jordan, and Egypt and in Latin America. The list goes on to include fifty countries.

In 2014 we introduced Bridges for Neighbors, a specialized course designed to reach the world's 1.6 billion Muslims, more than twenty percent of the world's population still waiting to hear the Good News of Jesus Christ. However now, 11,500 Muslim background believers (MBB's) in many countries have received Muslim-specific training and thousands are now hearing the Good News for the first time in oral forms that are relevant to Muslims. Though in our country some may view Muslim people groups with fear and misunderstanding, God sees them through a totally different lens. He loves Muslims and all people and "is not willing that any should perish". I say, "Look what God is doing". These are the accomplishments of God in a dark and broken world. I hope that it is clear to everyone that God is the author of it all and to God be the glory and honor. *After this I looked, and behold, a great multitude that no one could number, from every nation, from all tribes and peoples and languages, standing before the throne and before the Lamb, clothed in white robes, with palm branches in their hands, and crying out with a loud voice, "Salvation belongs to our God who sits on the throne and to the Lamb".* (Revelation 7:9-10)

As Jesus people, we must stay focused on reaching the unreached. This is the last great frontier. Consider the needs of oral learners throughout the world. Conservative estimates show over four billion people of the world are oral preference learners. Those who cannot read or simply choose not to read represent the most unreached and unengaged people across the globe with multitudes that have yet to hear and understand the Word of God. Hundreds of thousands of oral learners of many regions around the world have been reached and discipled but BILLIONS more still live in darkness. Currently, only 5% of fielded Christian missionaries are reaching the unreached. This is a shocking statistic. It is time that modern missions stop spending billions on the most reached countries and start working strategically among the least reached and training non-Western missionaries. I can envision hundreds of thousands of effective Special Operations teams, Jesus Units, men and women with unique callings going out in these later days.

I hope my story inspires others to follow their dreams, to cast the burdens and sins of the past, the obstacles of their upbringings, the pain and failure they have known and to call upon Jesus. They may become transformed men and women, knowing they are forgiven of their sins, following God and serving Him with all of their heart to the ends of the earth. In this century with the recent death of Billy Graham, many prophets, men and women of God are speaking out. It is a time for a new generation of Christian missionaries to be sent out and a Third Great Awakening to begin; young and old are committing their lives to missions in a call to action. Recently more than 40,000 gathered in Orlando Florida. 17,000 committed to a "Jesus Fast". Thousands have signed up to reach out to high school students and college-age young people. Others want to go to different nations to engage people with the gospel. Making Jesus famous throughout the world is on in the hearts of many. They are committed to His cause and many say the time is NOW for a massive missions wave to the unengaged and unreached, for a "New Jesus Movement." As I have relived my own journey through the writing of this book, I am inspired by the hope of such a new movement. My dream is that thousands find their calling in the coming days, months, and years and forge ahead in the service of the one and only God.

How Do I Get More Involved?

If this book has inspired you, get involved with a group that is focused on learning about God's heart for the nations through Bible storytelling, the Parables of Jesus, and adaptions to Scripture in song and dance. Below are additional resources that will help you to discover God's heart for the nations.

Pray for the Lord's clear discernment, direction and calling in your life and whether being a part of the orality movement is something that you could be a part of, bringing glory to His name and finishing the task of the Great Commission.

Additional Resources:

1. Book: Building Bridges to Oral Cultures by K. Carla Bowman & James Bowman
    www.missionbooks.org/collections/orality/products/building-bridges-to-oral-cultures

2. Feel free to explore SIU's free "Bridges Online" web-based orality exposure course by registering online for the course at any time at www.siutraining.org. This self-paced, basic entry-level course (which offers certification upon completion) gives you a taste of our equipping and training Bridges approach and methodology

3. Join our financial support team at Scriptures In Use. You can find our tax-deductible charitable giving options online at: www.scripturesinuse.org/give

4. Please review the **"Opportunities to Serve"** page at Scriptures In Use's website at www.scripturesinuse.org/serve/

5. Contact us at Scriptures In Use at www.scripturesinuse.org or 520.648.6400 and ask for Kent Kiefer. He can talk further with you about all of the opportunities available at SIU and the orality movement that is sweeping across the nations.

CPSIA information can be obtained
at www.ICGtesting.com
Printed in the USA
FSHW011847101019

9 781977 217875